Citizenship and Participation

ISSUES

Volume 175

Series Editor

Lisa Firth

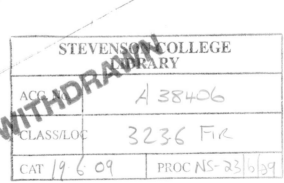
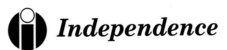

Independence

Educational Publishers
Cambridge

First published by Independence
The Studio, High Green
Great Shelford
Cambridge CB22 5EG
England

© Independence 2009

British Library Cataloguing in Publication Data
Citizenship and Participation — (Issues; v. 175)
1. Citizenship 2. National characteristics, British
3. Political participation — Great Britain
I. Series II. Firth, Lisa.
323.6-dc22

ISBN-13: 978 1 86168 489 9

Printed in Great Britain
MWL Print Group Ltd

Cover
The illustration on the front cover is by
Angelo Madrid.

CONTENTS

Chapter One: Identity and Belonging

Chapter Two: Democracy in Action

Chapter Three: Youth Participation

Useful information for readers

Dear Reader,

Issues: Citizenship and Participation

What does it mean to be British, and what makes a good citizen? This title covers what citizenship is, the rights and responsibilities of a citizen, our national identity and whether the concept of "Britishness" still has relevance in a modern society. It also looks at social participation and what it means to live in a democracy, including information on voting and government.

The purpose of *Issues*

Citizenship and Participation is the one hundred and seventy-fifth volume in the **Issues** series. The aim of this series is to offer up-to-date information about important issues in our world. Whether you are a regular reader or new to the series, we do hope you find this book a useful overview of the many and complex issues involved in the topic. This title replaces an older volume in the **Issues** series, Volume 131: **Citizenship and National Identity,** which is now out of print.

Titles in the **Issues** series are resource books designed to be of especial use to those undertaking project work or requiring an overview of facts, opinions and information on a particular subject, particularly as a prelude to undertaking their own research.

The information in this book is not from a single author, publication or organisation; the value of this unique series lies in the fact that it presents information from a wide variety of sources, including:

⇨ Government reports and statistics
⇨ Newspaper articles and features
⇨ Information from think-tanks and policy institutes
⇨ Magazine features and surveys
⇨ Website material
⇨ Literature from lobby groups and charitable organisations.*

Critical evaluation

Because the information reprinted here is from a number of different sources, readers should bear in mind the origin of the text and whether the source is likely to have a particular bias or agenda when presenting information (just as they would if undertaking their own research). It is hoped that, as you read about the many aspects of the issues explored in this book, you will critically evaluate the information presented. It is important that you decide whether you are being presented with facts or opinions. Does the writer give a biased or an unbiased report? If an opinion is being expressed, do you agree with the writer?

Citizenship and Participation offers a useful starting point for those who need convenient access to information about the many issues involved. However, it is only a starting point. Following each article is a URL to the relevant organisation's website, which you may wish to visit for further information.

Kind regards,

Lisa Firth
Editor, **Issues** series

** Please note that Independence Publishers has no political affiliations or opinions on the topics covered in the **Issues** series, and any views quoted in this book are not necessarily those of the publisher or its staff.*

What does citizenship mean?

Information from the Citizenship Foundation

The term 'citizenship' has several different meanings:

A legal and political status

In its simplest meaning, 'citizenship' is used to refer to the status of being a citizen – that is, to being a member of a particular political community or state. Citizenship in this sense brings with it certain rights and responsibilities that are defined in law, such as the right to vote, the responsibility to pay tax and so on. It is sometimes referred to as nationality, and is what is meant when someone talks about 'applying for', 'getting', or being 'refused' citizenship.

> **In its simplest meaning, 'citizenship' is used to refer to the status of being a citizen – that is, to being a member of a particular political community or state**

Involvement in public life and affairs

The term 'citizenship' is also used to refer to involvement in public life and affairs – that is, to the behaviour and actions of a citizen. It is sometimes known as active citizenship. Citizenship in this sense is applied to a wide range of activities – from voting in elections and standing for political office to taking an interest in politics and current affairs. It refers not only to rights and responsibilities laid down in the law, but also to general forms of behaviour – social and moral – which societies expect of their citizens. What these rights, responsibilities and forms of behaviour should be is an area of ongoing public debate, with people holding a range of views.

An educational activity

Finally, 'citizenship' is used to refer to an educational activity – that is, to the process of helping people learn how to become active, informed and responsible citizens. Citizenship in this sense is also known as citizenship education or education for citizenship. It encompasses all forms of education, from informal education in the home or through youth work to more formal types of education provided in schools, colleges, universities, training organisations and the workplace. At the formal end of the spectrum, it gives its name both to a distinct subject in the National Curriculum for 11- to 16-year-olds and to a general area of study leading to an academic qualification – both of which, confusingly, are sometimes spelled with a small and sometimes a capital 'c'.

⇨ Reprinted from *Making Sense of Citizenship: A Continuing Professional Development Handbook* (Hodder Murray, 2006), published by Hodder Education in association with the Citizenship Foundation, by permission of the publisher. For more information, visit the Citizenship Foundation website at www.citizenshipfoundation.org.uk

© *Hodder Education*

CITIZENSHIP

CITIZENSHIP EDUCATION

SOCIAL AND MORAL BEHAVIOUR

PUBLIC LIFE AND AFFAIRS

National ceremonies and symbols

The union flag, the national anthem, currency, stamps and other national events help identify and symbolise what it is to be British and to live in the United Kingdom

Flags

The Union Flag, or 'Union Jack', is the national flag of the United Kingdom and is so called because it embodies the emblems of the three countries united under one Sovereign – the kingdoms of England and Wales, of Scotland and of Ireland (although since 1921 only Northern Ireland, rather than the whole of Ireland, has been part of the United Kingdom).

The term 'Union Jack' possibly dates from Queen Anne's time (reigned 1702-14), but its origin is uncertain. It may come from the 'jack-et' of the English or Scottish soldiers; or from the name of James I (who originated the first union in 1603), in either its Latin or French form, 'Jacobus' or 'Jacques'; or, as 'jack' once meant small, the name may be derived from a royal proclamation issued by Charles II that the Union Flag should be flown only by ships of the Royal Navy as a jack, a small flag at the bowsprit.

The Department for Culture, Media and Sport provides information on how and when the Union Flag can be flown as well as information on which way up to fly it.

The Royal Standard represents the Sovereign and the United Kingdom. The Royal Standard is flown when the Queen is in residence in one of the Royal Palaces, on the Queen's car on official journeys and on aircraft. It may also be flown on any building, official or private (but not ecclesiastical buildings), during a visit by the Queen.

National anthem

'God Save the King' was a patriotic song first publicly performed in London in 1745, which came to be referred to as the National Anthem from the beginning of the nineteenth century. The words and tune are anonymous, and may date back to the seventeenth century. There is no authorised version of the National Anthem as the words are a matter of tradition.

Ceremonies

The armed forces are often involved in many of the great ceremonies of state. The Army website gives details of events such as trooping the colours, the state opening of Parliament, Remembrance Sunday and state visits.

Currency, coins and banknotes

The Bank of England has issued banknotes since it was founded in 1694. Its website provides information on the history and design of banknotes.

The Royal Mint can be traced back more than a thousand years and is still a department of government. Its main responsibility is the provision of the United Kingdom's coinage. The Mint's website sells coins and related collectables.

The UK remains outside the Euro area. The Treasury runs a website to provide information on the Government's work to ensure that the UK could make a smooth and cost effective changeover to the Euro, if that is what Government, Parliament and the people, in a referendum, decide.

Stamps

The Royal Mail publishes stamps for the UK.

Symbols of the royal origins of the UK's postal system remain: a miniature silhouette of the Monarch's head is depicted on all stamps.

Great Seal

The Great Seal of the Realm is the chief seal of the Crown, used to show the monarch's approval of important state documents. In today's constitutional monarchy, the Sovereign acts on the advice of the Government of the day, but the seal remains an important symbol of the Sovereign's role as Head of State.

Royal Coat of Arms

The function of the Royal Coat of Arms is to identify the person who is Head of State. In the UK, the royal arms are borne only by the Sovereign. They are used in many ways in connection with the administration and government of the country, for instance on coins, in churches and on public buildings.

The coat of arms are familiar to most people as they appear on the products and goods of Royal Warrant holders.

The Royal Coat of Arms being displayed on a public building

The Crown Jewels

The crowns and treasures associated with the British Monarchy are powerful symbols of monarchy. For over 600 years kings and queens of England have stored crowns, robes and other valuable items of ceremonial regalia at the Tower of London. Since the 17th century, at least, this collection has been known as the 'Crown Jewels'.

⇨ The above information is reprinted with kind permission from Directgov. Visit www.direct.gov.uk for more information.

© Crown copyright

'Moaning, drinking and queuing' make us British

Britain's national traits include getting drunk, moaning and taking pleasure in the misfortune of others, according to a survey that paints a grim picture of our culture

Our top national characteristic is talking about the weather, just ahead of a passion for queuing, but other qualities in the top ten are not so endearing; sarcasm, a love of television soaps and curtain twitching were all identified as central to the British identity.

Obsession with class was also high on the list, along with more modern ills such as pandering to political correctness and road rage.

Working long hours, fascination with property prices and the love of bargains also made it into the top 50, suggesting that our behaviour during the financial crisis may be more ingrained than we think.

But it was not all bad news. Stiff upper lip came out at number eight in the poll, with respondents also picking out a reluctance to complain, good sense of humour and the ability to laugh at ourselves.

The results were based on a study of 5,000 adults who were asked to pick out the things – good and bad – they believe make us unique as a nation.

A spokesman for global research company OnePoll.com, which conducted the survey, said that despite some of the negative traits identified, Britons were still extremely proud of their country.

By Matthew Moore

'This is a brilliant list of characteristics and some of the observations are absolutely spot on,' he said.

'You can't go anywhere or do anything in Britain without someone talking about the weather, and we're almost proud of the fact that we get more rain than anywhere else.

'What this poll demonstrates really well is how proud we are to be British – more than two-thirds of respondents said they felt honoured to be a part of this country.'

Top 50 'typically British' traits

1 Talking about the weather.
2 Great at queuing.
3 Sarcasm.
4 Watching soaps.
5 Getting drunk.
6 A love of bargains.
7 A love of curtain twitching.
8 Stiff upper lip.
9 Love of all television.
10 Moaning.
11 Obsession with class.
12 Gossiping with neighbours over the garden fence.
13 Obsession with the traffic.
14 Enjoying other people's misfortune.
15 Inability to complain.
16 Love of cheap foreign holidays.
17 Working long hours.
18 A soothing cup of tea to ease worries.
19 Eating meat and two veg.
20 Looking uncomfortable on the dance floor.
21 Feeling uncomfortable when people talk about their emotions.
22 Clever sense of humour.
23 Obsession with property values.
24 Pandering to political correctness.
25 Road rage.
26 Being unhappy with our weight.
27 Wanting a good tan.
28 Being proud of where we live.
29 Not saying what we mean.
30 The ability to laugh at ourselves.
31 Washing the car on a Sunday.
32 Taking the mickey out of others.
33 Asking people about their journey.
34 Inability not to comment on how other people bring up their children.
35 Jealousy of wealth and success.
36 Being overly polite.
37 Texting instead of calling.
38 An inability to express our emotions.
39 Obsession with the Royal Family.
40 Fondness for mowing the lawn.
41 Love of rambling through the countryside.
42 A love of all things deep fried.
43 Emulating celebrity lifestyles.
44 Leaving things to the last minute.
45 Irony.
46 Keeping our homes neat and tidy.
47 Take decisions and accept the consequences.
48 Achieving against all odds.
49 Wanting our sportsmen/teams to fail.
50 DIY on a Bank Holiday.

10 November 2008

A more United Kingdom

Should we have a day to celebrate what we like best about Britain?

A national day of celebration is an idea that is unashamedly civic. In debates about creating new spaces and places to reinforce the things we have got in common, a national day has come to the fore. Last year, Ruth Kelly and I published an argument that it was time to think about a 'Britain Day', and we offered the example of the success of Australia Day as a model. As I went around the UK talking to the public about shared standards and how we celebrate them, I could not resist asking too what people thought of a Britain Day.

'British Day is a great idea to raise awareness of being British and celebrating having a British passport, no matter what your culture'

I was impressed at the strength of support I heard. Not that it was to everyone's taste. Indeed the views I heard approximated the balance reflected in a Home Office poll we took last year, in which broadly two-thirds expressed support with around 25 per cent against, the balance saying 'I don't know'.

Let me start with the case against – the negative views. Among some was a suspicion that this was an idea that was simply an invention of the government: 'its just a talking point for politicians' or, worse, '[it] feels like a government gimmick to reunite a disunited country' to make good for the fact that citizens today 'don't feel British', and that the idea was only being proposed because 'our culture has been diluted and our country fragmented'. Or simply: 'It's too late to bring this in.'

Others argued:

'There are no communities now to celebrate in; we don't know [our] neighbours so [are] unlikely to celebrate with them.'

'Britain is not Britain any more – lost its values – how can we celebrate when it doesn't really mean anything?'

'Unsure what "Britain Day" would mean – we don't know what British is as we're trying too hard to take into account other cultures and religions.'

Mixed into this was a different but related idea, that trying to celebrate something in common was simply too difficult:

'Not sure about themes – these are already covered by Armistice Day and scouts/guides.'

'[The] most defining thing about Britishness is multiculturalism, diversity, sharing and understanding other cultures – can't manufacture a sense of togetherness out of this.'

'Different parts of UK would have different view of what should happen and when – may be divisive or cause animosity.'

Others had different concerns. Some did not like the idea that a national day might be something 'forced' – 'you can't force people to celebrate'. Feared one: 'Britain Day would be a way to get people to conform', and another put it bluntly: 'I would drink at the pub – it's my right to do what I want on the day.'

Some worried that the day would alienate people – and that everyone would want a day for themselves or that any such day would have to be 'multicultural day' because there would be too much disagreement about what the day should look and feel like as it was forced to take account of our citizens' many different backgrounds. And there was a flip side to this argument, a suspicion that the celebration would not in fact be a celebration of our country: 'Political correctness would mean [being] unable/not allowed to celebrate truly British things, [to] fly [the] British flag.'

The final fear was of gratuitous wastefulness. Some did not feel we needed a national day to have a celebration. The cost would end up coming from taxes and having a bank holiday would (negatively) affect employers. The money could be better used in specific communities. The UK already has lots of public holidays and opportunities to do things together (like participating in the Children in Need appeal – but Christmas, bonfire night and Halloween were also mentioned) and people 'would just go on holiday' with another day off. Annually might be too often – once every five years was posed by one as an alternative. And one or two participants fretted that public holidays are commercialised and people would try to make money out of it (although some thought this was a positive).

This was, however, the minority view. The positive argument predominated in the discussions I listened to – but it was difficult to put a finger on why Britain Day was an appealing idea. It was partly because people wanted the space to make a statement about what they loved about the UK. It reflected a comment I heard in a discussion with my own constituency party, which is ethnically very mixed and where we have had a series of arrests in recent, high-profile counter terrorism operations: 'We want the media to see the unity in the community.'

Around the country, people echoed this sense that the UK has always been a pretty diverse place and because of this there has evolved an extra need to raise awareness about our shared history and values of tolerance, as well as simply to celebrate the things of which we are proudest (the military and the NHS are often mentioned).

So, people talked about raising awareness of our national history, and creating ways of bonding between different communities, something many felt we were particularly good at

precisely because Britain is a collection of nations linked into one nation that is not actually defined in terms of a single ethnic race or religion:

'British Day is a great idea to raise awareness of being British and celebrating having a British passport, no matter what your culture.'

'[It would be] a way to bond people of different nationalities [and] bring communities together, similar to Notting Hill Carnival [and] the Mela in Hyde Park.'

'[The] event would help to remind people that being British is about helping each other out, being in the community, inclusiveness.'

'Celebrating Britain would help people appreciate it and learn more about it and previous generations.'

'[It would be] an opportunity to celebrate historical events.'

'A national day would bring together more people, [an] opportunity to mix.'

'[It would] give people a sense of belonging.'

'[It would be] an opportunity to celebrate Britain. [It would be] a way to educate others about Britain.'

'[It would] help people to understand cultures of different parts of the UK.'

Some also felt a national day would have a positive impact on integration. On the one hand it could help newcomers feel welcomed, but more importantly it would help people understand what it means to be British. As one participant put it: 'We need to define this and it is very diverse because it also means allowing people to celebrate their own culture.' A national day would help people

learn about and accept cultural and social differences between each other, while also providing some space to talk about the history of Britain – and about the changes in the country.

People had some clear ideas, too, about how we should celebrate. I had this debate initially with my own local Labour Party in Hodge Hill, Birmingham, in 2007. Overall, among my own party members, there was strong support for the idea of a Britain Day. There was a strong sense that the day was so important that it should be a public holiday – but there was no consensus about when it should be, although there was a strong feeling it should be separate from Remembrance Sunday. This lack of consensus was mirrored in the discussions I had around Britain. The list of suggestions for when a Britain Day might be held included:

⇨ on the Queen's birthday;
⇨ on May Day;
⇨ on All Saints' Day;
⇨ on a day with historic significance, e.g. Hastings Day, Trafalgar Day, Magna Carta Day, Empire Day;
⇨ in the summer – to allow for outdoor celebrations;
⇨ on St George's Day (others disagreed) or other saint's day;
⇨ by making more of an existing day, e.g. Pancake Day, Whitsunday or Easter.

Other suggestions were to have a national day held in London, with local events elsewhere, that a bank holiday would encourage people to get involved in; to hold the event over a weekend, and to hold it during a day and evening but not as a week-long event. My own preference would be a

day in late Spring (the last Monday in May is already a day off everywhere) – or to agree a day at the beginning or the end August (which means either a new day for Scotland, or England, Wales and Northern Ireland depending what was agreed).

My own party members wanted a happy – rather than a mournful or solemn – day, which had space for expression and celebration of the wonderful diversity of British life, woven with opportunities to come together in a celebration of what we have in common. They wanted to see colour and celebrations of costume – what we called 'kilts and saris' with a strong emphasis on celebrating foods – traditional and new. Hodge Hill members were keen on local, neighbourhood celebrations, like street parties, before coming together in broader civic gatherings: the proverbial 'Party in the Park'.

Across the UK, some wanted a carnival to get everyone involved; others felt that carnivals are not British. People put lots of different ideas for locations to me:

⇨ in the local park;
⇨ in central London;
⇨ at Buckingham Palace;
⇨ in Trafalgar Square;
⇨ in Hyde Park;
⇨ in Portsmouth dockyard;
⇨ in schools;
⇨ in community centres;
⇨ at university;
⇨ at the same venue as where there are Christmas lights.

Members were not keen on placing too much emphasis on the 'trappings of nationalism', by which they meant too much emphasis on 'saluting flags'. They wanted the media to see 'the unity within the community' but a community that also celebrated the 'colours of the British tapestry'. Around Britain, people had many similar ideas, reflecting perhaps a very healthy lack of order.

September 2008

⇨ The above information is an extract from the Demos report *A more United Kingdom* by Liam Byrne, and is reprinted with permission. For more information or to view the full report, visit www.demos.co.uk

© *Demos*

Citizens feel a strong sense of belonging

Information from the Department for Communities and Local Government

People feel their local area is a place where individuals from different backgrounds get on well together, new figures published today show (29 January 2009).

Headline figures from the citizenship survey show that 82 per cent of people see their community as cohesive, an increase from 80 per cent in 2005.

Also:

⇨ 76 per cent of people feel that they strongly belong to their neighbourhood, with 81 per cent of people satisfied with their local area as a place to live;

⇨ older people were more likely to be satisfied with their local area than younger people (88 per cent of people aged 75 years and over).

The survey is less positive on people feeling their voices are being heard at a local level. Fewer than 40 per cent of respondents felt able to influence decisions in their local area. This is an area the Government is keen to address and has set out plans – in its *Communities in Control* White Paper and in new legislation currently in Parliament – which will go even further in giving more power to local people.

Cohesion Minister Sadiq Khan said:

'Britain has a proud history of individuals from different backgrounds living side by side with each other and as this survey shows there remains more uniting us than dividing us.

'We must not take this for granted though. We need to ensure that Britain continues to be a place where people are proud to live and everyone can succeed. That means building on what we have already done to deliver equal opportunities and racial equality.

'Too few people feel they can influence decisions either at a local or national level. This is something we must address and why we are giving people more power to have a greater say in the way that local decisions that affect them are made.'

These findings come from *The Citizenship Survey: April-September 2008* (covering the first two quarters of data from the 2008-09 survey).

Every year almost 15,000 people are asked for their views on issues around community cohesion, discrimination, values, civic engagement and interaction. The biggest survey of its kind in the UK, the survey is one of the key tools used by Government to measure the effect of its policies.

The full survey is available on the Communities and Local Government website. Among the key findings are:

Community cohesion and belonging

⇨ 76 per cent of people felt they belonged strongly to their neighbourhood, an increase from 70 per cent in 2003;

⇨ 81 per cent of people were satisfied with their local area as a place to live;

⇨ older people were more likely to be satisfied with their local area than younger people. Levels of satisfaction were highest among those aged 75 years and over (88 per cent) and lowest among those aged 16 to 24 years old (76 per cent);

⇨ 81 per cent of people mixed socially at least once a month with people from different ethnic or religious backgrounds.

Active and empowered communities

⇨ 39 per cent of people feel they can influence decisions affecting their local area. 22 per cent feel they could influence decisions

affecting Great Britain. Both measures remain unchanged since 2007/08 but both have fallen since 2001;

⇨ 41 per cent of adults have volunteered formally at least once in the 12 months prior to interview.

Discrimination

⇨ 10 per cent of people said that racial or religious harassment was a big problem in their local area. A higher proportion of people from minority ethnic groups (20 per cent) thought that racial or religious harassment was a problem compared to White people (nine per cent);

⇨ eight per cent of people from minority ethnic groups felt they had been refused a job for reasons of race compared with two per cent of white people who felt they were refused a job on these grounds.

29 January 2009

⇨ The above information is reprinted with kind permission from the Department for Communities and Local Government. Visit www. communities.gov.uk for more information.

© Crown copyright

Statistics on citizenship

Statistics from the Department for Communities and Local Government's Citizenship Survey, April-September 2008, England

Whether people feel able to influence decisions affecting their local area and Great Britain, 2001 to April-September 2008

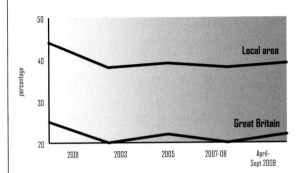

Participation in civic engagement and formal volunteering at least once in the last year, 2007-08

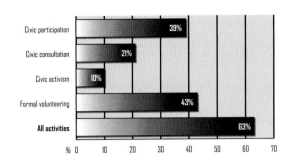

Percentage agreeing that their local area is a place where people from different backgrounds get on well together, by ethnicity

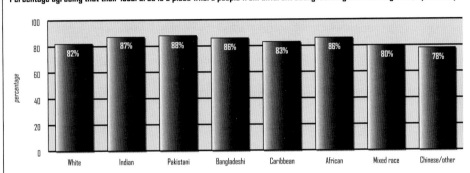

White 82% Indian 87% Pakistani 88% Bangladeshi 86% Caribbean 83% African 86% Mixed race 80% Chinese/other 78%

Mixing with people from different ethnic or religious backgrounds by ethnicity (percentage mixing at least once a month), 2007-08 and April-September 2008

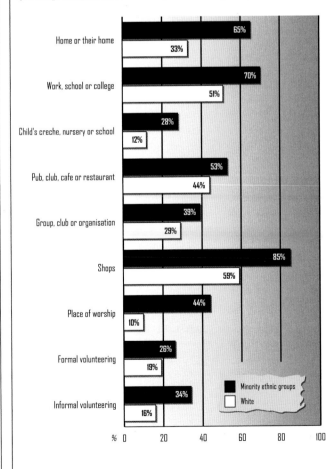

Whether racial or religious harassment is a problem in the local area, April-September 2008, by ethnicity

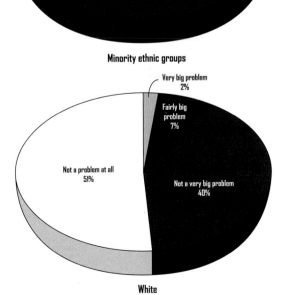

Minority ethnic groups

White

Source: 'Citizenship survey April-September 2008, England', Department for Communities and Local Government, January 2009. Crown copyright.

Citizenship: our common bond

Lord Goldsmith recommends new emphasis on the common bond of citizenship

In his report *Citizenship: Our Common Bond*, published today, former Attorney General Lord Goldsmith sets out reforms that will make it clearer what it means to be a citizen and practical measures that may help to enhance a sense of shared belonging.

Lord Goldsmith said:

'It is easy to imagine that British citizenship should denote a strong connection with membership of the community in the UK; that British citizenship denotes a strong commitment to, and connection with, this country. However, that is not historically the case.

'In effect, the history of legislation on citizenship and nationality has led to a complex scheme lacking coherence or any clear and self-contained statement of the rights and responsibilities of citizens.

'My report discusses measures to address that and makes a range of proposals that touch every stage of an individual's life. My recommendations are intended to promote the meaning and significance of citizenship within modern Britain.'

The report contains key findings from a five-month investigation into the current condition of citizenship in the UK. To make it clearer who is a citizen and what it means to be a citizen it recommends:

⇨ abolishing residual types of citizenship, with the exception of British Overseas Territories Citizenship and British Nationals Overseas status, to allow people who qualify for those categories to obtain full British citizenship;

⇨ providing that only citizens should have the fullest rights to political participation. The right to vote of non-citizens should be phased out while retaining the rights of EU citizens living in the UK and Irish citizens who have

Irish citizenship by connection to Northern Ireland;

⇨ reforming the category of permanent resident as it blurs the distinction between citizens and non-citizens. We should expect people who are settled in the UK for the long-term to become citizens and recognise those who cannot do so (because their country of origin does not allow dual nationality) as Associate Citizens;

⇨ reform of the law of treason to make the duty of allegiance relevant to modern conditions.

To enhance our sense of shared belonging along all stages of a citizen's journey through life, the report recommends:

⇨ creating a clear statement of the rights and responsibilities of citizenship, which we have never had in the UK;

⇨ developing a new national day which becomes a focus for expressing our sense of shared belonging. The national day will provide a framework in which different communities in different parts of the UK come together to celebrate their common bonds;

⇨ building the common narrative through citizenship education – which the report proposes should be an element of primary education as well;

⇨ that citizenship education has to be active throughout, consisting in learning through doing;

⇨ young people should be launched towards full participation in society through a citizenship ceremony at the end of school;

⇨ reduction in university fees for those who take part in civic activities;

⇨ a new standard to give employers an incentive to promote civic engagement among their workers – Investors in Communities;

⇨ creating more mentoring opportunities for people at different stages of their lives – including mentoring relationship between young and old.

The report also looks at how to engage newcomers to the UK in UK society. That means:

⇨ taking new steps to promote the learning of English – including language loans for people who cannot afford to pay for lessons at the outset;

⇨ a mentoring scheme for people aspiring to become citizens;

⇨ encouraging more people to take a citizenship course through which they will have the opportunity to talk about what citizenship means with other people;

⇨ using citizenship ceremonies to connect new citizens with the local community – for example, by involving local schools, community organisations and cultural institutions.

Lord Goldsmith was asked by the Prime Minister last year to conduct the review as part of changes proposed in the Governance of Britain green paper.

11 March 2008

⇨ The above information is reprinted with kind permission from the Ministry of Justice. Visit www.justice.gov.uk for more information.

© *Crown copyright*

British identity

Its sources and possible implications for civic attitudes and behaviour

In the last decades of the twentieth century, there was a decline in the proportion of people in Great Britain who thought of themselves as primarily or exclusively British and a growing proportion of people who thought of themselves as Scottish, Welsh or English (or none of these) rather than British.

A sense of British identity nevertheless remains widespread and in all three territories the majority of British residents continue to have dual identities, as both British and Scottish, British and Welsh or British and English. A small but growing number (around 10%) of people reject all four national identities.

Britons tend to feel proud of being British, and levels of national pride are higher than in most other countries in the EU15. In contrast, levels of attachment or sense of belonging to Britain (which may be the more relevant aspect in the context of civil society) is below the European average.

There is evidence of decline over the last two decades in strength of national pride (although largely from 'very strong' to 'fairly strong' sense of pride) and there may well have been a modest decline in attachment too.

The main driver of a feeling of attachment or belonging to Britain is age, with younger people being less strongly attached to Britain. It is likely that much of the decline in pride and attachment is generational in character, with younger generations who feel a lower sense of attachment gradually replacing older generations.

Controlling for age, we find no evidence that Muslims or people of Pakistani heritage were in general less attached to Britain than were other religions or ethnic groups. Ethnic minorities show clear evidence of 'dual' rather than 'exclusive' identities. However, people born overseas in a non-Commonwealth country and people who have arrived in Britain only recently tend to have a weaker sense of belonging to Britain.

Socio-economic marginality (lower social class or low income, or a limiting long-term illness) is associated with slightly weaker feelings of belonging.

Among young people born in Britain, the lack of attachment of Black Caribbeans is especially marked, reaching one-third or more. This applies to the second generation as well as to the first, migrant generation.

A feeling of belonging or attachment to Britain appears to be associated with social trust, a sense of civic duty (at least as indicated by turnout in elections) and by increased support for the current political order. However, in international comparisons Britain does not rank especially highly on measures of social trust, social participation or sense of civic duty.

A sense of belonging to Britain is not associated with particularly xenophobic attitudes, nor is it associated with distinctive political positions (other than on European integration and maintenance of the union) or with many other aspects of social participation or values. However, there is some evidence that it is associated with an 'ethnic' rather than a 'civic' conception of the nation.

The predominant conception of Britain is one that sees both ethnic (such as ancestry) and civic (such as respect for political institutions) criteria as important. Ethnic conceptions tend to be somewhat backward looking, taking pride in Britain's history, and tend to be exclusive. Primarily civic conceptions of the nation tend to be more inclusive, and countries that have more strongly civic conceptions also exhibit high levels of 'good citizenship'.

The evidence base is not yet sufficiently strong for firm policy recommendations. But policies should, perhaps, be considered which address the weak sense of belonging on the part of people born overseas in non-Commonwealth countries, of second-generation minorities (especially those of Caribbean heritage) and of the economically marginal. These policies might well include both 'direct' ones aimed at strengthening national identity and 'indirect' ones aimed at tackling some of the root causes of lack of belonging.

Any reforms need to consider not only how to strengthen British identity but also what form of identity should be encouraged.

By Professor Anthony Heath and Jane Roberts

⇨ The above information is the executive summary of the Ministry of Justice document *British identity: its sources and possible implications for civic attitudes and behaviour* and is reprinted with permission. Visit www.justice.gov.uk for more information or to view the full report.

Britishness and social cohesion

Trying to create a fixed sense of 'Britishness' will not achieve social cohesion

Addressing deprivation and how people connect is more important for social cohesion than trying to get everyone to adhere to the same fixed notion of 'Britishness'. This is according to research published today (21 July) by the Joseph Rowntree Foundation. The report also found that limited opportunities for British people in parts of the UK are undermining attempts to ensure new migrants are well received. It found a stark divide between places that are equipped to adapt to new migrants, and places that are not.

The research, *Immigration and social cohesion in the UK*, found that many people valued their children growing up with cultural diversity. However, some felt that their, and their children's, prospects were reduced because of immigration – particularly when it came to housing and education.

Lead Researcher Professor Mary Hickman, Director of the Institute for the Study of European Transformations (ISET) at London Metropolitan University, said: 'We found that although many British people value the UK for being multi-ethnic and multicultural, poverty and lack of opportunities undermine social cohesion, especially in certain parts of our towns and cities. A key factor influencing whether new migrants are accepted is the dominant story in each locality about who belongs there.'

Communities who saw their locality as belonging to everyone tended to be more open to new arrivals. Whereas communities who thought of a locality as belonging to them in particular were more likely to blame new arrivals for problems that often already existed.

The report also looked at feelings of Britishness among both the settled UK population and new migrants in England, Scotland and Northern Ireland. It found that minority ethnic long-term residents and new arrivals were the most positive about what was good about Britain.

White English people who were questioned often found it difficult to reflect on their feelings of belonging to Britain, because they had not previously considered it. Whereas people in Scotland and Northern Ireland felt they belonged more to their respective nations than to Britain.

The authors conclude: 'The find-ings of this research go against the grain of the idea that we need a fixed notion of Britishness and British values. Rather, 'cohesion' is about negotiating the right balance between difference and unity.'

This press release summarises information from the Joseph Rowntree Foundation report Immigration and social cohesion in the UK *by Mary Hickman, Helen Crowley and Nick Mai. 21 July 2008*

⇨ The above press release is reprinted with kind permission from the Joseph Rowntree Foundation. Visit www.jrf.org.uk for more information.

© Joseph Rowntree Foundation

A question of identity

Are you Scottish or British?

By David Leask

Scottish? Or British? For generations many Scots were happy to be a bit of both. Now, for the first time, they will officially have to decide between the two.

The Scottish Government yesterday published the likely questions on national identity for the next census. People living in Scotland in 2011 will be asked to tick one of 21 boxes that they think best defines their ethnic or national background. There will be a box for 'Scottish' and a box for 'British' but none for both.

Government statisticians want to get to the bottom of who the residents of Scotland think they are. Polls have persistently shown most people living in Scotland feel more Scottish than British. But what will they say when they have to make up their mind between two identities that are exclusive rather than complementary?

'I'll put British,' said Bill Aitken, a veteran Tory and Unionist who it would be hard to mistake for anybody but a native Glaswegian. 'I am a British Scot. This is clearly the Scottish Government trying to drive a wedge between Scotland and the rest of the UK. While we are all proud of our Scottishness, we are British as well. This is just a juvenile attempt to create divisions where they don't exist.'

London-born and English-accented Nigel Don, a fellow MSP, has a different take. 'I would put myself down as Scottish,' the Nationalist said. 'I have never had any doubts about that, regardless of where I was born. And that would not be a political answer.'

The Scottish Parliament will have to give its blessing to the census forms before they are used. But the proposed new questions on national origins will be used by the Scottish Government for a whole range of purposes, including its efforts to monitor the ethnic background of people who apply for public-sector posts. The reason: to ensure nobody is discriminated against on racial grounds.

'A national identity question is also being tested and developed for the census and relevant Scottish Official Statistics,' a spokeswoman for the Scottish Government explained. 'This will let people express their national identity fully – be that Scottish, British or any other national identity – before expressing their ethnicity. The Registrar General is developing a question for publication in autumn 2008.'

The last census, in 2001, also quizzed people about their ethnic origins, but only offered 14 options. The first, for people who categorise themselves as White, was 'Scottish', the second 'other British', allowing Scots who felt British to put 'Scottish' without denying their Britishness. Whites could also choose to be Irish or Other White.

Now there are far more options. First is 'Scottish'. Then come 'English', 'Welsh', 'Northern Irish', 'British', 'Irish', 'Gypsy/Traveller', 'Polish' and 'Any Other White Ethnic Group'.

The form will also include another 12 boxes, for people of Asian, African and Caribbean or other descent, including, for the first time, a subcategory for people who identify themselves as Arabs.

Rob Wishart, Scotland's Chief Statistician, said: 'Since the last census in 2001, Scotland has become a more ethnically-diverse country. So it is vital that the next census (in 2011), and other Scottish Official Statistics, provide good information about different ethnic groups in Scotland.

'That will help ensure that public services are geared to everyone's needs and that any discrimination is detected.

'To do that effectively, we need to ask the right question in the census and other Scottish Official Statistics. We have consulted a lot of people and held useful discussions,

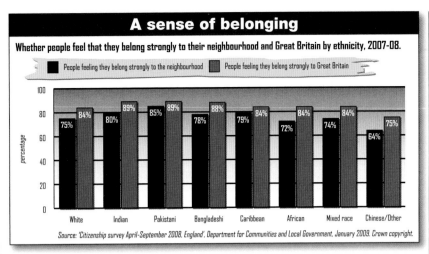

A sense of belonging

Whether people feel that they belong strongly to their neighbourhood and Great Britain by ethnicity, 2007-08.

■ People feeling they belong strongly to the neighbourhood ■ People feeling they belong strongly to Great Britain

White: 75%, 84%
Indian: 80%, 89%
Pakistani: 85%, 89%
Bangladeshi: 78%, 88%
Caribbean: 79%, 84%
African: 72%, 84%
Mixed race: 74%, 84%
Chinese/Other: 64%, 75%

Source: 'Citizenship survey April-September 2008, England', Department for Communities and Local Government, January 2009. Crown copyright.

as well as testing a wide range of possible questions. We believe that we have chosen a question which people can understand and answer easily, but which also allows people to record their ethnicity in the way which best suits them and provides the information which is needed to tackle discrimination and inequality.'

The decision to review ethnic classifications in statistics was first ordered by the then Labour-LibDem administration in 2002. The Equality and Human Rights Commission has, so far, endorsed the decision. The Office of National Statistics will decide how it will count people's ethnic and national identity later.

Some Labour politicians were yesterday bristling about the wording of the questions, however. Frank McAveety, a Labour MSP and one of hundreds of thousands of Scots of Irish ancestry, warned the end results of any such census question wouldn't say very much about Scotland's appetite for independence.

He said: 'Statistics could misrepresent who people think they are. I am Scottish and I am British but if I had to state a preference, I would say I am Scottish.'

What will we find out?

⇨ Just how strong Scottish identity is. For the first time we will know how many Scottish residents, regardless of their views on the constitution, regard themselves as first and foremost Scots.
⇨ How many English people live in Scotland. Previous censuses and surveys have asked how many people see themselves as not

Scottish but British and how many people were born in England. The new model will pinpoint the exact number of people who regard themselves as being English, by far the biggest minority national group north of the border.

_____

Polls have persistently shown most people living in Scotland feel more Scottish than British

_____

⇨ How many Poles have come to Scotland. There is remarkably little robust information on the exact number of people to come to Scotland from Poland – and other parts of Eastern Europe – since they were given the right to live and work here in 2004.
⇨ The new questions won't, however, measure how many Scottish residents of Asian, African or other ethnic backgrounds regard themselves as, say, 'Scottish Asian' rather than 'British Asian'. Bluntly, people who regard themselves as white have to decide whether they are Scottish or British. People who define themselves as Asian, African or of other minority groups can't do so, even if they wanted to.
31 July 2008

⇨ Reproduced with the permission of the Herald & Times Group. Visit www.theherald.co.uk for more information.
© _Herald & Times Group 2008_

Britain and beyond

Between May and July 2008, YouthNet carried out research to explore young peoples' attitudes towards diversity in the UK, European citizenship and issues such as immigration, multiculturalism, integration and racism

YouthNet is the UK's first exclusively online charity and runs two award-winning websites: the guide to life for 16- to 24-year-olds, TheSite.org, and the UK's volunteering database, do-it. org.uk.

Between May and July 2008, YouthNet carried out research to explore young people's attitudes towards diversity in the UK, European citizenship and issues such as immigration, multiculturalism, integration and racism. This project was funded by the Youth in Action Programme.

Using an online survey and an online focus group discussion, YouthNet consulted with more than 850 young people from across the UK aged between 16 and 24.

British and European identities

⇨ The focus group participants were fairly ambivalent about being described as British and did not readily relate to a shared British identity. They were, however, conscious of the nations which made up the UK, both culturally and in terms of personal identity.

⇨ For many of the young focus group participants, the concept of 'Britishness' consisted of a variety of cultural stereotypes and associations, both positive and negative. They identified more readily with the idea of accepting change and difference, which some perceived to be a British quality.

⇨ Around half (51%) of the survey respondents said they feel European; however, the vast majority (74%) thought that the UK was very different to the rest of Europe.

⇨ Perceived cultural differences, more than geography, dissuaded many young British people from identifying as European. These included food, eating habits, art and a difference in attitudes on the continent to binge drinking.

⇨ Nearly half (46%) of the survey respondents considered themselves to have good knowledge of European cultures, having acquired it from friends, holidays and the media. Only a quarter (27%) thought that young people were taught a lot about other European cultures at school.

Going abroad

⇨ Nearly nine in ten (87%) young British people who took part in the survey had visited countries in Europe outside of the UK. Over half (56%) had been abroad beyond Europe.

⇨ Over half (56%) of the survey respondents who had visited another European country generally felt safe in European countries. Almost one in twenty (17%) did not.

⇨ Three out of five (62%) survey respondents believed that Europeans were welcoming to British visitors, and two in five (44%) said that the British were not discriminated against in European cultures.

⇨ A significant minority (13%) of respondents said that Europeans were not welcoming to British visitors, and some focus group participants believed that being British, or moreover English, was the reason for negative attitudes towards them.

⇨ Less than half (46%) of the survey respondents spoke a European language other than English and many felt that language barriers caused difficulties for them in European countries.

⇨ Many focus group participants were aware of a stereotyped British failing to learn other languages. Many felt self-conscious about this and ashamed of their inability to fully communicate while abroad.

Influencing UK attitudes to Europe

⇨ On the whole, the young British people who took part in the research were not anti-Europe or the EU; however, most felt that UK media coverage of the issues was largely negative.

⇨ Focus group participants were concerned that negative media stories about Europe unfairly influence people's attitudes and create hostility towards the EU and immigration, and encourage racist behaviour.

⇨ They also said they would like to see more informed and varied coverage about Europe and the EU in order to inform and develop their own opinions.

⇨ Two-thirds (67%) of the survey respondents watched films made in European countries other than the UK, while the same proportion (68%) listened to European music.

⇨ Focus group participants said they wanted to see more European films shown in mainstream cinemas.

⇨ Many were hopeful about the future of the UK's relationship with Europe and the EU, although they were concerned about widespread ignorance and negativity about the issues. They suggested schools, the media and the Government could address this.

⇨ The above information is an extract from the YouthNet research *Britain and beyond* and is reprinted with permission. Visit www.youthnet.org to view the full report.

© *www.youthnet.org*

Just who do we think we are?

A review published this week by the former attorney general Lord Goldsmith said that more than a third of young black Britons feel no sense of attachment to Britain, while a further one in ten people said they rejected all four identities of British, English, Scottish or Welsh. Among other ways to enhance British bonds, Goldsmith suggested extending citizenship ceremonies to all 18-year-olds, with an oath of allegiance to the Queen or to the country. Across the country the Guardian went on to the streets to ask how British people think they are.

Bradford

Three union flags were hanging high over Bradford's Centenary Square, wrapping themselves limply round their poles in the way that the emblem of the country is apt to do. Down below, enthusiasm for a post-school oath of allegiance was equally lukewarm, but not because of any hesitations about feeling naturally British.

'It's just that there's no point in it. I think it's a waste of time,' said chef Ali Umma, 30. 'Wasting public money, too. We're already running a good system as it is, so why do they need to introduce new things like this?'

He and his friends on a lunch break accepted there were problems between communities, but he said: 'Which country doesn't have those? We can solve them, maybe quicker if we use the money they'd be wasting on this allegiance thing.'

Royalty was likely to be a particular sticking point for younger people, as older ones in the square acknowledged. Susan Rhodes, retired from a career in social care, said: 'You wouldn't get young people to do it. Maybe in our day, but times have changed.'

Stephen Smith, 28, a scrap-yard worker said: 'The Queen'd be the sticking point for me. I'm not against her or anything, but she's not special. She's just like the rest of us, or should be. Not someone you swear an oath to.'

Three students from Bradford College worried that the suggested ceremony could be more divisive than helpful. Laura Barker, 17, said: 'It's just going to divide people more, because the ones that will swear allegiance are going to be mad at people that don't, or don't want to. They're going to have to make it like you have a choice, because so many people will just leave if you have to do it.'

Her friend Chantelle Brooking, also 17, agreed and echoed Umma: 'We've got on so well before without it, so why bother? People are going to unify whether we have an oath of allegiance or not. It's not any symbol that's going to bring us together, it's people getting together.'
Martin Wainwright

Stirling

When Audrey Ferrand was looking for a name for her luxury Scottish goods shop in the centre of Stirling, she wanted something that reflected her identity as a Scot and a Briton. She opted for Thistle & Rose. Ferrand, 42, who was born in South Lanarkshire, lived and worked in London and Paris for 15 years before returning to Scotland with her French husband to raise their children.

'I think I would say I am British first and then definitely Scottish - probably the Scottish side has got a stronger feel to it. Scottish people have always been proud of being Scottish, but I don't think devolution or the parliament has made a great difference to us, in terms of having an even stronger identity. We are still British first.'

Ferrand said she would accept that the notion of Britishness had dissipated in recent years but did not believe that the government could counter it with initiatives such as a national day or an oath of allegiance to Queen and country. 'Absolutely not,' she said. 'It's more about the way we live and who we are.'

James Mackay, 55, from Dunkeld, a retired RAF flight engineer, spent 23 years in the air force and worked on the Queen's Flight, including the monarch's 1991 visit to Africa. As a member of the armed forces he was required to swear an oath of allegiance, and had no issue with doing so. But he is vehemently opposed to ministers intervening to promote the notion of Britishness, particularly making school leavers swear an oath of allegiance to Queen or country.

'I think it's terrible, it's absolutely diabolical. I think getting children to swear allegiance to the Queen is appalling. I am totally against it.' Mackay said he was a Scot who was proud to be British, but suspected that many Scots would baulk at efforts by Westminster to cultivate a renewed sense of Britishness. 'I don't think this whole thing will go down very well here,' he said. 'It is a very nationalistic country, Scotland.'

Roy Smith, 42, an auxiliary nurse at Stirling Royal Infirmary, said people were taking the issue too seriously.

'I'm Scottish. If you go to America and people say, 'oh you're English,' I always correct them. But if someone was to call me British it would not bother me,' he said.

'And I don't think there is really a problem about Britishness. The politicians are thinking too much about it. We have a multicultural society now, which is a good thing about the UK. We should focus on that.'

John Wood, 23, a restaurant manager, agreed. 'It is not government's place to tell us how we should be feeling. People have the right to form their own opinion.'

Kirsty Scott

Jermyn Street

On Jermyn street, leaning on his cane a thimble's throw from Piccadilly, stands a bronze statue of that icon of understated nattiness, George 'Beau' Brummell. His personal and very British credo – 'To be truly elegant one should not be noticed' – is engraved on the plinth beneath his boots. And while it may be hard to know what Brummell would have made of Lord Goldsmith's proposals, the shoppers and vendors of Jermyn street had their own ideas.

'Getting children of 18 to swear allegiance to the Queen is a gimmick,' said John Bray, who was also happy to provide a brutal appraisal of Goldsmith's sartorial shortcomings outside his menswear shop. 'The trouble with this country is that the politicians are like advertising men: they're trained to lie with enthusiasm.'

Bray, 73, describes himself as 'very much British' and feels that a sense of national identity is best forged at home.

'It would be much better if the parents brought them up in all aspects of life,' he said. 'My wife is Polish and I spend quite a lot of time in Poland. The children over there treat their elders very differently from the way they do here. Education starts at home.'

Felix Cole, 49, a financial adviser, was equally uncharitable about some elements of the citizenship review – especially the mooted oath. 'I thought it was nuts,' he said. 'It's an American idea and I don't think it would work here. I just feel that it's every parent's job to bring up their kids and give them personality and character and show them the country they're living in. It's not the state's responsibility.'

By 18, he added, young people should have developed an understanding of their country and their

place in it. However, Cole, who considers himself English despite the odd drop of Scottish and Irish blood, does feel more should be done to highlight the richness of the national identity. 'That's the thing about the British character; we have influences from all over the world. I'm always surprised by how many Indians were killed fighting for England – though you never hear about them.'

Walking past Turnbull & Asser was Jane Brackfield, who had more time for the oath, but harboured reservations about the wording and what young people would think about it. 'It would be very nice if people did it with their families because families are a big thing in this country.'

Should British teenagers be asked to swear an oath of allegiance to the Queen?

'I think we mustn't be afraid to let people practise what they want to practise,' she said. 'I've got no problems with people celebrating other things but I don't feel that I should be ashamed of saying I'm a Christian. It would be nice if we could have Muslims, Jews and Christians all saying the same thing and swearing allegiance to the country they live in and embracing it.'

Not everyone could see what all the fuss was about. 'I think you already have a good sense of national pride,' said Justine Hartman, 23, who came to Britain from Johannesburg three years ago. But the foreign exchange accountant felt that national identity was less about flags and oaths than welcoming the young into their own country.

'If everyone said the oath was a great idea, it would be fine, but I think the kids will just think it's a gimmick. I think it's really about making the

younger generation feel more a part of society and not being pointed at and told that they're bad. In South Africa, you feel proud and excited to be young, but here it's just about who's been shot, who's been stabbed. They don't give them a chance from the get-go.'

Colin Barlow, 55, a motorcycle taxi driver from Kent, pondered Britain and Britishness as he waited for a fare outside Dolce & Gabbana on Old Bond Street. 'I think it's going to the dogs,' he said. 'We're losing our identity and there's less pride in being British these days. It's a very slow process; these things don't just stop, but politeness is disappearing a bit and people are getting a bit more aggressive.'

'The Americans, for example, have a culture of being proud of being American, and if we had that, it would be better.' He was, however, in no doubt as to his own identity. 'I'm English,' he said. 'I've always lived here and I can't speak Welsh - or understand the Scots.'

Sam Jones

Thetford

The Norfolk market town of Thetford is home to an estimated 10,000 Portuguese drawn to East Anglia by the promise of well-paid work on the farms, in fields and in the factories.

Most have arrived in the past seven years to begin a new life in a community of Norfolk locals and London overspill.

The town was the birth place in 1734 of Thomas Paine, a passionate defender of the Rights of Man – the title he gave his polemic against the monarchy – and his statue dominates the main street.

And the European arrivals who now throng the same street would doubtless endorse republican Paine's view that income tax from the rich should be used to provide education, pensions and unemployment benefits.

Bar manager Helder Lopez – whose pub was attacked by stone-throwing white locals after Portugal knocked England out of the World Cup two years ago – said: 'I have been here seven years and I consider myself British. I have two young sons and a daughter and they all speak English as well as Portuguese. I would be happy for them to take an oath of allegiance to this country but the final choice will have to be theirs.'

'But too many people come here thinking it is easy street – and for many that turns out to be true. I know people from Europe who have come to this town and haven't had a job in five years. For them it is a land of milk and honey, but for the rest of us it has sometimes been a struggle. Most of us have learned the language so we can feel included in the life here yet too often the scroungers don't do anything and don't join in.'

Joao de Noronha is editor of a Thetford-based Portuguese newspaper published fortnightly with a national circulation of more than 20,000 – 2,000 copies of which are sold in Thetford.

He believes language is the barrier to closer integration of the Portuguese in Thetford. He says most of the under-30s arrive – especially those of school age – and learn English quickly. But he admits the older generations, some of whom have been here for seven years, are not prepared to change.

He has helped to set up European Challenge, an organisation dedicated to helping new arrivals settle in the area by offering translation and interpretation services and practical guidance to bureaucracy in the UK.

Naronha, 57, said: 'There is a problem with language which we are trying to address and it has been a barrier. Older people do not see themselves as included and they do not wish to be. But the younger ones want to be included so they have mixed emotions.

'Most of us would have no problem with swearing an oath of allegiance – this country is now their home and they do not want to go back to Portugal.'

Not everyone in Thetford, however, sees the benefits of the mass immigration. Derek Antrobus and his wife, Maureen, moved to the town 34 years ago to escape city life in the north of England. In that time they say they have seen plenty of change – enough for them to claim they feel like foreigners in their own land.

Mrs Antrobus, 57, said: 'I feel we are now in a minority here. Walking through the town all you hear is foreigners – they have their own shops, pubs and cafes, which is not a bad thing. I have got some Portuguese friends but it is not the same sleepy Norfolk town it was when we arrived.'

Mr Antrobus, 71, said: 'The Europeans came here to work in the fields and factories probably, but over the years not enough has been done to make provision for them. Our housing, health and education systems have struggled to cope with such an influx of foreigners who all want to live and work here.'
Richard Goss
⇨ Originally published in *The Guardian*, 15 March 2008.
© *Kirsty Scott*

Citizenship tests

Information from HeadsUp!

Since 1 November 2005 everyone that wants to permanently live in the UK has to take a test or attend citizenship and language classes to prove that they know about life in the UK.

The Home Office said it wanted to create a new, more meaningful way of becoming a citizen to help people share British values and traditions. Tony McNulty, the Immigration Minister at the time the tests were introduced, said:

'This is not a test of someone's ability to be British or a test of their Britishness. It is a test of their preparedness to become citizens, in keeping with the language requirement as well. It is about looking forward, rather than an assessment of their ability to understand history.'

The subjects in the test are:

1 A Changing Society (migration, the role of women, children, family and young people);
2 UK Today: A Profile (population, the nations and regions of the UK, religion, customs and traditions);
3 How the United Kingdom is governed (the British constitution, the UK in Europe and the world);
4 Everyday needs (housing, services in and for the home, money and credit, health, education, leisure, travel and transport);
5 Employment (looking for work, equal rights and discrimination, at work, working for yourself, childcare and children at work).

The test is made up of 24 questions which have to be answered in 45 minutes in English. You need to get 18 out of the 24 questions right to become a British Citizen - would you?
October 2008

⇨ The above information is reprinted with kind permission from HeadsUp! Visit www.headsup.org.uk for more information.
© *Hansard Society*

Parliament and the public

Knowledge, interest and perceptions. By Susanna Kalitowski

What does the public think about Parliament?

The Westminster Parliament is the heart of representative democracy in the United Kingdom. Its own brand of parliamentary democracy, the 'Westminster system,' has been replicated around the world. The Palace of Westminster, with its iconic bell tower and dramatic position on the banks of the River Thames, is one of the most recognisable buildings on earth – an international symbol of the UK, as well as a physical embodiment of democracy.[1]

But what do the British people think about the illustrious institution which represents them? There is evidence that public confidence in Parliament has been rapidly declining over the past several decades.[2] The Hansard Society's annual *Audit of Political Engagement* has recently found that only a third of the population is satisfied with how the institution works.[3] In an effort to shed further light on the complex relationship between Parliament and the public, the Hansard Society commissioned a survey examining public attitudes towards the institution.[4] This report presents our findings, which are grouped into three categories:

⇨ Knowledge and understanding of how Parliament works and the distinction between Parliament and government;

⇨ Interest in Parliament and the desire to know more about it;

⇨ Perceptions of whether Parliament is important, relevant, accessible, representative and is generally working for people.

Key findings

The results of the survey reveal strikingly low levels of knowledge about Parliament as well as some surprising perceptions about its role as an institution. The key findings include:

⇨ Just 32% of people agree that they 'have a good understanding of the way Parliament works';

⇨ Only one in two members of the public are confident that Parliament is not the same thing as government;

⇨ Over half of people (53%) have an interest in Parliament, although nearly as many (47%) have little or no interest;

⇨ Around one in two (47%) are interested in learning more about Parliament;

⇨ Younger people (aged 18-34) and women are more likely to want to know more about Parliament, while people from lower social grades are far more likely to say they would not like to know more;

⇨ Nearly half of people agree that Parliament undertakes important functions that no other body can undertake and a majority feel it is relevant to their lives;

⇨ An overwhelming majority of people feel that Parliament is unrepresentative of British society;

⇨ Only 19% of people agree that Parliament is 'working for them'.

Some of these findings – particularly vis-à-vis knowledge and understanding – are unquestionably troubling. On a more positive note, others suggest that, contrary to popular belief, most people are not completely apathetic about Parliament. A majority of the public appear to have an interest in and a high regard for the institution even if it does not currently live up to their expectations and ideals.

Notes

1 Winston Churchill dubbed the House of Commons the 'shrine of the world's liberties'. Winston Churchill quoted in P. Hennessy, 'An end to the poverty of aspiration? Parliament since 1979', unpublished paper, November 2004, p. 23.

2 For example, MORI research found that trust in Parliament dropped from 54% in 1983 to 14% in 2000. See M. Woolf, 'Cameron launches taskforce to "restore trust in politics"', *The Independent*, 5 February 2006.

3 Hansard Society & Electoral Commission (2007), *An audit of political engagement 4* (London: Hansard Society and Electoral Commission), p. 7.

4 This publication is based upon a Hansard Society report for the Group for Information to the Public (GIP) of the Houses of Parliament, *Removing Barriers to Engagement*. The Hansard Society commissioned ComRes to poll 1,023 UK adults by telephone between 4 and 5 June 2008. The data was weighted to represent the national distribution by age, region and gender.

June 2008

⇨ The above information is reprinted with kind permission from the Hansard Society. Visit www.hansardsociety.org.uk for more information.

© *Hansard Society*

Parliament sits in the Palace of Westminster in London

Discover Parliament

Information from UK Parliament

What is Parliament?

The Parliament of the United Kingdom consists of:

⇨ the House of Commons (646 elected Members of Parliament or MPs);

⇨ the House of Lords (approx-imately 720 unelected members, most of them appointed for life);

⇨ the Queen (our hereditary monarch).

What does Parliament do?

Parliament is responsible for making and changing the laws of the United Kingdom and for checking (scrutinising) the work of the Government.

Why do we need Parliament?

We live in a democratic country, which means that we can all have a say in how the country is run. We do this by electing MPs to represent our views in the House of Commons; the part of Parliament which has the greatest political power. The expertise and independence of members of the House of Lords complement the work of the House of Commons.

What is devolved Government?

To give the people of Scotland, Wales and Northern Ireland more say over what happens in their own countries, the UK Parliament has devolved (given away) some of its powers to other national and regional bodies. In Scotland, for example, there is the Scottish Parliament which has elected members who make some decisions for Scotland. Wales and Northern Ireland also have their own Assemblies. A Greater London Assembly has also been established.

Parliament and Government

What is the Government?

The Government is like the management of the country. It is made up of about 100 members of the political party which wins the most seats at a general election and so has the most MPs in the House of Commons. Most of those in the Government will be MPs but some will be members of the House of Lords.

What is the difference between Parliament and Government?

While the job of Government is to run the country, the job of Parliament is to check Government is carrying out its role properly and effectively. To do this, Parliament has powers to limit the Government and prevent it from becoming too powerful. Government is accountable to Parliament for all of its actions.

The House of Commons

What is the House of Commons?

The House of Commons is made up of 646 Members of Parliament (MPs) who are elected by the voters (the electorate) to each represent an area of the UK which is known as a constituency. We all live in a constituency and have an MP to represent us in the House of Commons.

MPs represent all of the people who live in their constituency, whether or not they voted for him or her.

What does the House of Commons do?

The main functions of the House of Commons are:

⇨ to pass laws;

⇨ to provide (by voting for taxes) the money which the Government needs to carry out its work;

⇨ to check (scrutinise) that the Government is doing its work properly;

⇨ to debate the major issues of the day.

Where does the House of Commons meet?

The House of Commons meets in a special chamber within the Palace of Westminster in London.

Who's who in the House of Commons?

The leader of the political party with the most seats (MPs) in the House of Commons (the governing party) becomes Prime Minister. He or she chooses a number of senior members of their party to become ministers. Ministers sit on the front bench in the House of Commons, so are known as frontbenchers. They lead debates and answer questions about their departments from the despatch box.

The party which has the second largest number of seats in the House of Commons is known as the Official Opposition.

Its leader is known as the Leader of the Opposition and will also choose senior members of his or her party to be shadow ministers. They sit on the front bench opposite the Government so are known as Opposition or Shadow frontbenchers.

All of the other smaller parties are known as Opposition parties even though some may support the Government.

All of the MPs who are not either ministers or Shadow ministers are known as backbenchers.

Who are Whips and what do they do?

Each party chooses a number of its MPs to be Whips. Whips are responsible for making sure that all members of the party know what is going on and know who to go to if they have a problem. They are also responsible for party discipline.

Each party issues its Members with a weekly timetable of what is happening in the House of Commons and gives guidance as to how the party hopes its Members will vote on issues. This timetable is also known as the Whip. Votes (divisions) are underlined once, twice or three times according to how important the party thinks that the issues are. All MPs are expected to be present to vote on issues which are underlined three times (a three-line whip) unless they have special permission from their Whip to be absent.

Who keeps the House of Commons in order?

The House of Commons can be a very noisy place where lots of MPs have very strong views and may all want to speak in a debate. It is the job of the Speaker to keep order in the Chamber and to make sure that as many MPs as possible are able to take part in the debate.

The Speaker is an experienced MP who is chosen by all of the other MPs to be their Speaker at the beginning of each Parliament. Once chosen, the Speaker must give up all party views and be politically impartial so that he or she can be fair to all. The Speaker's most well known words are 'Order, Order' and all MPs, even the Prime Minister, must obey him or her.

What does the House of Commons do?

Making laws

New laws are needed to deal with our constantly changing society, hence the House of Commons spends nearly half of its time making new laws which are known as Statute Laws. Laws are made in different ways for example, some are made by the European Union because when we joined in 1973 we agreed to obey European laws. Some of our laws have developed over hundreds of years from decisions made by judges in law courts – these are known as Common Law.

Debates

The House of Commons is where major issues of the day are debated with different arguments being put forward and opinions given. In this way all MPs have the chance to express their concerns and make their views, and those of their constituents, known. At the end of a debate MPs give their opinion by voting either aye (yes) or no.

Controlling money

The Government needs money in order to be able to run the country. It raises this from taxes. Each year, usually in March or April, the Government minister responsible for finances, the Chancellor of the Exchequer, makes a statement to the House of Commons in which he explains how he intends to raise the money which the Government needs to spend. This is known as the Budget. The House of Commons has a duty on behalf of the people of the country to make sure that the Government is not raising taxes without good reason and is spending the money wisely.

Examining the work of the government

Parliament has a duty to keep a check on (scrutinise) the work of the Government. It does this in a number of ways.

Select committees

Select committees in the House of Commons check the work of government departments. There is a committee for every major department. Committees are usually made up of 11 MPs who meet together to conduct enquiries into areas of the work of their particular department. They can take written evidence and ask for witnesses to come and answer questions, usually in public. At the end of an inquiry the committee publishes a report which everyone can read and which may be debated in Parliament. This means that questions are always being asked about the work of departments and attention can be drawn to matters

How laws are made

No new law can be made unless it has completed a number of stages in both the House of Commons and the House of Lords and has been signed by the monarch. A proposed new law is known as a Bill and can only become an Act of Parliament, and the law of the land, once it has completed all of its stages.

Preparatory stages

Before a bill is introduced, those people who are likely to be affected may be consulted and discussion documents, called Green and White Papers, may be produced. Sometimes a bill is published in draft form so that it can be debated by a select committee in its early stages.

House of Commons

First Reading

The bill is first introduced into Parliament so that people know that it is coming up for discussion.

Second Reading

This is a very important stage where the minister in charge will explain the purpose of the bill and answer questions. All MPs can attend the debate and vote on the bill.

Committee Stage

Most bills are considered by a small group of between 15 and 50 MPs in a Standing Committee. Here the bill can be examined in detail and changes (amendments) can be made.

Report Stage

Any amendments made by the committee are reported in the Commons for all MPs to consider. New amendments may also be introduced at this stage.

Third Reading

MPs vote for the final time as to whether they want the bill to progress or not. If they agree the bill goes to the House of Lords for them to consider.

House of Lords

First Reading

The bill from the Commons is announced in the House of Lords.

Second Reading

This is the main debate on the bill.

Committee Stage

This is where detailed clause-by-clause examination of the bill takes place. All members of the House of Lords can participate and amendments can be proposed.

Report Stage

This is a further chance to change the bill.

Third Reading

Last chance for discussion and, unlike the Commons, to make further amendments.

Royal Assent

Once both Houses have agreed with each other's changes then the bill goes to the monarch for Royal Assent. It can then become the law of the land as an Act of Parliament.

Note: Bills can begin in either House (above, the bill is assumed to have started in the House of Commons). Bills which start in the Lords go through the same stages.

of concern. The Government must respond to each report although it is not bound to accept the committee's recommendations.

Question Time

Question Time takes place for almost an hour on Mondays to Thursdays. Ministers are responsible for the work of their departments and must answer questions about once a month. Any MP can apply to ask an oral (spoken) question but there will not be time for all of them to be answered. Questions can also be answered in writing. In this way ministers, including the Prime Minister, are answerable to the House of Commons for their work.

The Opposition

Opposition parties can question the work of the Government and have set times when they can choose the topics for debate. The Official Opposition mirrors the Government with its Shadow Cabinet and presents alternative policies so that voters have a choice at election time. On international matters and at times of crisis the Opposition will often agree with the Government and offer its support.

The House of Lords

What is the House of Lords?

The House of Lords is the second chamber in the United Kingdom's Parliament. It has approximately 720 members. Members of the House of Lords together have great breadth of expertise and, individually, are characterised by independence of thought. They complement the work of the House of Commons by making laws, scrutinising the Government and providing independent expertise.

What does the House of Lords do?

Makes laws

All bills must be agreed by both Houses of Parliament before receiving Royal Assent and becoming law. All bills that come from the House of Commons will be reviewed and some bills will start their life in the Lords.

If the Lords make changes that the Commons do not like then the bill will go backwards and forwards between the two until agreement is reached. If they cannot agree then the Lords can only delay the passage of a bill for about a year. This is because the House of Commons is our elected House and its wishes take precedence.

However, the House of Lords can stop a bill to extend the life of a Parliament beyond five years to make sure that an unpopular Government cannot delay elections to stay in power.

Examines the work of the Government

Parliament has a duty to scrutinise the work of the Government. The House of Lords does this in a number of ways.

Debates

The House of Lords holds debates which give a valuable opportunity to discuss matters of public interest or to talk about a report which has just come out. These debates draw on the members' wide range of knowledge and expertise. In times of crisis special debates will be held in the Lords at the same time as in the Commons.

Question Time

Government ministers in the Lords have to answer questions about their work as in the Commons. Question Time takes place at the beginning of each sitting day for about half an hour. Questions can also be asked and answered in writing.

Provides independent expertise

Like the Commons, the Lords have select committees. The main difference is that, instead of looking at the work of government departments, Lords' select committees deal with broader issues such as scientific, economic and constitutional affairs. They also have a major role in scrutinising European laws. When a committee finishes its work on a particular matter it publishes a report for the House to debate and for the public to see what it has discovered.

Judicial work

The House of Lords is currently the highest court in the land. If the judge in a lower court is unsure about a point of law it can be referred through higher courts until it reaches the House of Lords. This judicial work is carried out only by highly qualified judges called Law Lords. From 2009 this legal function will be removed completely from the House of Lords. A new UK Supreme Court will replace the House of Lords as the highest court of appeal in the country. As the members of the House of Lords are not elected they have no power over how our taxes are raised and spent. Parliament's work on these matters is all done by the House of Commons.

What types of Lords are there?

Currently there are four types of Lords:

Life peers

Most of the members of the House of Lords are life peers. They are appointed by the monarch on the advice of the Prime Minister for the duration of their lives, often for services to the country. This ensures a wide range of expertise amongst the membership of the House of Lords.

Hereditary peers

The House of Lords Act 1999 effectively removed the right of peers who inherited their titles from their family to sit and vote in the House except for 92. The 92 who remain are no longer able to pass on to their children the right to sit as a member of the House of Lords.

Law Lords

The country's most senior judges, known as Lords of Appeal in Ordinary, are appointed to the House of Lords, which is, until 2009, the highest court in the land.

Bishops

The 26 most senior Archbishops and Bishops of the Church of England are members of the House of Lords.

Where does the House of Lords meet?

The House of Lords meets in a special chamber at the opposite end of the Palace of Westminster to the House of Commons. The seats in the House of Lords are red.

How is the House of Lords organised?

The House of Lords is organised on a party basis in much the same way as the Commons with all the major parties, together with some of the smaller parties, being represented by peers. The Government sits on the benches on the right side of the throne with ministers sitting on the front bench. Opposition members sit opposite with the shadow ministers sitting on their front bench. Most senior ministers are members of the House of Commons but most government departments will have one minister who is a member of the Lords to answer questions and to speak for his or her department.

Who keeps the House of Lords in order?

Members of the House of Lords are more orderly and polite than MPs so do not need anyone to keep them in order. In the Lords, the Leader of the House is the leader of the governing party and gives advice to all peers. The Lord Speaker sits on the Woolsack. Her role is very different from that of the Speaker in the House of Commons as she does not keep order and does not decide who should speak next.

Who are the Whips and what do they do?

As in the House of Commons the parties in the House of Lords appoint Whips to be their business managers and to help with communication. Party discipline is not so strong in the House of Lords as members are more independent.

The Government

What is the Government?

The Government is chosen by the leader of the political party which has the majority of seats in the House of Commons. It is made up of about 100 MPs and members of the House of Lords who become government ministers.

The Conservative party won the general election in 1979, 1983, 1987 and 1992 so we had a Conservative Government for 18 years. The leader of the governing party becomes the Prime Minister so we had Margaret Thatcher and then John Major as Conservative Prime Ministers. Since Labour's election victories in 1997, 2001 and 2005 we have had a Labour Government.

What is the Cabinet?

The Prime Minister chooses about 20 senior members of the Government to form the Cabinet. The majority of members of the Cabinet come from the House of Commons but there will also be a few members from the House of Lords. Heads of government departments and other senior figures such as the Lord Chancellor will normally be included in the Cabinet but the final decision rests with the Prime Minister. The Cabinet usually meets on a Thursday morning in private in the Cabinet Room at 10 Downing Street. It decides on which policies should be introduced at what time and how the Government should respond to what is happening.

What are Government Departments?

The work of the Government is divided between departments of state which each specialise in a particular subject, such as the Home Office or the Department of Health. The minister in charge of a government department is usually a Cabinet minister and is often called a Secretary of State. He or she may have been chosen for his or her special interest in, or knowledge of, the subjects handled by the Department and will make all the important decisions affecting the Department. The Secretary of State will be helped by one or more junior ministers.

Although the majority of members of the Government belong to the House of Commons, most departments will have one minister who sits in the House of Lords. As well as their work within their departments, ministers have to speak and answer questions on the work of their department in Parliament.

Robert Walpole is today regarded as the first British Prime Minister, holding office from 1721 to 1742

Who are civil servants?

Ministers may not stay in their departments for very long and all will change if a new Government is chosen at election time. They are helped in their work in their departments by officials who are known as civil servants. Civil servants are not members of political parties and serve each Government. They may spend years in one department and have time to become experts in their work or to develop technical skills which are needed to run services throughout the country such as the benefits system.

Ministers rely on civil servants for information and advice when working out policies but must be the ones who make the final decisions as they, and not the civil servants, are accountable to Parliament and the people.

The Monarchy

In the United Kingdom we have a hereditary monarchy which means that the title passes from one member of the royal family to another – usually to the eldest son, or if there are no sons, to the eldest daughter, as was the case with Queen Elizabeth. Our current royal family is the House of Windsor.

At one time the monarch was very powerful and ruled the country. Gradually the people wanted to have some say in how the country was run. The current House of Lords developed from the council of wise men who were chosen to give advice to the monarch.

Later, members of the House of Commons were elected by the people and gradually took political power from the monarch. Today the majority of the powers which were previously exercised by the monarch are carried out either by or on the advice of the Prime Minister and the Government, making the monarch what is known as a constitutional monarch.

Many people such as life peers, ministers, senior members of the church and judges are officially appointed by the monarch, but it is on the advice of the Prime Minister. The monarch has to give Royal Assent to all bills but this is done as a formality and has not been refused since 1707. Although the Queen opens each session of parliament and reads the speech from the throne, it tells us what the Government hope to do in the next year, and has been written by the Prime Minister. In this way important decisions are made by those people who are elected to represent us.

The Queen is able to provide the Government with the benefit of her knowledge, as she deals with many officials and foreign leaders. She can also offer advice based on past experience, having so far worked with 10 different Prime Ministers.

⇨ The above information is reprinted with kind permission from UK Parliament. Visit www.parliament.uk for more information.

© Crown copyright

Modern Britain 'needs Parliamentary reform'

Commission calls for reforms to make Parliament fit to represent modern Britain

Trevor Phillips, Chair of the Commission, will argue that our political institutions need radical reform or Parliament faces losing its legitimacy, when he gives evidence to the Speaker's Conference today.

The Speaker's Conference was established in November 2008 to make recommendations for bringing the representation of women, ethnic minorities and disabled people in the House of Commons more in line with the population at large. At present, only 15 of the 646 MPs are black or Asian, and women make up just 19 per cent of MPs.

The Commission fears that the routes people follow into Parliament are being narrowed due to the professionalisation of politics and the metropolitan bias towards those who can take unpaid internships. The Commission will therefore undertake research into the pathways MPs follow into the House of Commons with a view to identifying barriers which may exist for under-represented groups. The Commission is recommending that Parliament considers introducing an internship scheme so more people from diverse backgrounds can gain experience working for Members of Parliament.

The Commission is also proposing that the Speaker's Conference considers the implications of limiting the number of terms MPs and Lords can serve and enhancing the House of Lords Appointments Commission to include political appointments.

Trevor Phillips says: 'The Commission starts from the position that a Parliament which reflects the make-up of the nation it represents will result in better legislation and a higher degree of public confidence in the democratic process.

'Political parties have a major role to play in promoting diversity, and it is up to them how they run their own selections. Local party members don't set out to vote against a woman or a black man. But like most other people many members have an image in their head of what a politician looks like. If you asked a class of children to draw a picture of a politician then the chances are nine out of ten would draw a picture of a white man in a grey suit.

Voting turnout has dropped to record lows in recent general elections

---

'That assumption doesn't leave us when we get older. In a selection meeting anyone who doesn't fit this image has a mountain to climb before they even open their mouths. This stereotype will be self perpetuating unless parties take action to break the mould.'

A recent Ipsos MORI poll published by the Commission shows that British people are increasingly comfortable with racial diversity. 40 per cent of 16- to 24-year-olds from an ethnic minority background think there is more racial tolerance than ten years ago. However, they lack faith in political institutions to treat everyone fairly. Voting turnout has dropped to record lows in recent general elections, illustrating that many people – particularly the young and ethnic minorities – do not think that Parliament reflects and acts on their concerns.

While there is a commitment across all political parties to increase the diversity within Parliament, the current rate of change in the House of Commons in particular is incredibly slow.

The Commission believes that one way of speeding up turnover would be to impose a term limit for MPs. Limiting MPs to serving a maximum of four parliamentary terms – or roughly 20 years – would allow more people from a wider range of backgrounds to enter the House. These limits could also be considered for the House of Lords. However the proposals would need careful consideration as, for example, it would be important to ensure time limits didn't prevent Parliament benefiting from the experience of long-serving members.

The Equality and Human Rights Commission argues that a quick way to achieve a more representative second chamber would be to enhance the role of the House of Lords Appointments Commission to include political party recommendations as well as independent nominations. The Appointments Commission could then work with the parties to ensure that nominations increase diversity in the chamber rather than reduce it.

Finally, in its submission, the Commission points out that many other public bodies – for example the Police, Armed Forces, legal and teaching professions – as well as many private companies, have changed their recruitment processes to better reflect society and their customers. Parliament should look for examples of good practice from these organisations. These could include mentoring and role models, flexible working, and an internship scheme for sixth formers or graduates such as those operating in Washington or Brussels for young people from disadvantaged backgrounds.
3 March 2009

⇨ The above information is reprinted with kind permission from the Equality and Human Rights Commission. Visit www.equalityhumanrights.com for more information.
© Equality and Human Rights Commission

Parliamentary elections

Elections allow citizens to determine how the country should be governed

What is an election?

In an election those eligible to vote (the 'electorate') select one or more options – usually a person or a political party – from a list of candidates. This article concentrates on the election of Members of Parliament (MPs) to the House of Commons, but in the United Kingdom regular elections also take place for the Scottish and European Parliaments, the National Assembly for Wales, the Northern Ireland Assembly, the Greater London Authority (and directly elected Mayor of London) and for local government (county and district councils, unitary authorities, etc).

Why have elections?

Fair and free elections are an essential part of a democracy, allowing citizens to determine how they want the country to be governed.

General elections

What is a general election?

A general election is held when Parliament is dissolved by the monarch on the advice of the Prime Minister. General elections must be held at least every five years. All seats in the House of Commons are vacant and the political party that wins the most seats in the Commons in the subsequent general election forms the government.

Political parties

What are political parties?

A political party is a group of people who seek to influence or form the government according to their agreed views and principles. It is not always easy to distinguish between political parties and pressure groups. Essentially a political party will have policies to cover all general areas of public policy, whereas a pressure group will seek to influence one specific policy area, for example the environment.

Why do we need political parties?

Political parties are essential to provide voters with a free choice between options. They help to organise public opinion on national matters, they provide a permanent link between Parliament and the electors and they provide stability and cohesion in Parliament.

Which political parties do we have in the United Kingdom?

The Westminster Parliament has traditionally been dominated by the two party system, with two main parties forming the Government and the Official Opposition. Over the years these have been Whigs and Tories, Liberals and Conservatives and, since the development of the Labour Party at the beginning of the twentieth century, Labour and Conservatives. A number of other parties have also won seats in Parliament. After the 2005 election the Liberal Democrats were the third largest party with 62 seats.

Candidates

Who can stand as a candidate in a general election?

Any person who is a British, Commonwealth or Irish Republic citizen may stand as a candidate at a parliamentary election providing he or she is aged 21 or over.

Those disqualified from sitting in the House of Commons are:

1 Members of the House of Lords including those bishops who are Lords Spiritual.
2 Undischarged bankrupts.
3 Offenders who have been sentenced to more than 12 months imprisonment, during the period they are detained (or unlawfully at large).
4 Persons convicted of illegal or corrupt practices at elections (disqualified for seven years).
5 Those holding offices listed by the House of Commons Disqualification Act 1975 (such holders need to be politically impartial whilst carrying out their jobs) including: senior civil servants, judges, ambassadors, members of the regular armed forces, members of the police force, paid members of the boards of nationalised industries, government-appointed directors of commercial companies and directors of the Bank of England.

What happens if a disqualified person stands successfully in a general election?

In the event of a disqualified candidate standing successfully in a general election the person is unable to take his or her seat in the House of Commons and the defeated opponent may apply to have the election declared null and void.

How are candidates chosen?

Any eligible person can become a candidate whether or not he or she belongs to a political party. Anyone who wishes to stand for election must be nominated on an official nomination paper giving his or her full name and home address. They must stand either for a registered political party or as an independent; it is no longer possible to give a description on the ballot paper unless the candidate is standing for a registered political party. The nomination paper must include the signatures of ten electors who will support him or her, including a proposer and a seconder. Candidates must consent to their nomination in writing. All candidates must pay a £500 deposit which is lost if they do not secure 5% of the total number of votes cast in their constituency and is set at this level to discourage large numbers of frivolous candidates from standing. The nomination papers and deposit must be submitted to the Returning Officer in each constituency during a specified period in the election campaign.

However, to stand a realistic chance of being elected to the Commons under our present system, a candidate needs to represent one of the three main political parties in Great Britain or a nationalist or unionist party in Scotland, Wales or Northern Ireland. Each party has its own method of selecting candidates.

Why does a person with no realistic chance of being elected stand as a candidate?

The fact that almost anyone can stand for Parliament is one of the essential freedoms in our democracy and provides voters with a choice. Publicity is a key factor for individuals: they may gain national publicity like the late Screaming Lord Sutch and his Monster Raving Loony Party, local publicity for a particular issue or cause about which they feel strongly, or for themselves as an individual.

Voters

Who is able to vote in parliamentary elections?

All British, Irish and Commonwealth citizens are entitled to register to vote in elections to the House of Commons providing they are 18 or over and are not disqualified in any way. Irish and Commonwealth citizens must be resident in the UK. Those who are unable to vote are:

1 Members of the House of Lords.
2 Those detained in mental hospitals.
3 Prisoners who have been sentenced to more than 12 months imprisonment, during the period they are detained (or unlawfully at large).
4 People convicted within the previous five years of corrupt or illegal practices during elections.
5 Citizens of the European Union and countries other than those of the Commonwealth and Republic of Ireland even if they are tax paying or long-term residents.
6 People who on polling day cannot make a reasoned judgement.

This is very different from the situation in the early 19th Century when only around three adults in every hundred were eligible to vote. The 'franchise' (the right to vote) has been gradually extended over the past two centuries. For example, the Representation of the People Act 1918 allowed, for the first time, most women over 30 to vote, and the Representation of the People Act 1969 lowered the age at which people could vote from 21 to 18.

How do I ensure that I can vote?

You can only vote if your name appears on the electoral register. This is updated on a monthly basis and, if you move, you should alert your new local Electoral Registration Officer. Each autumn, there is also a canvass of every household to check eligibility to vote. The householder must give details of all occupants who are eligible to vote, as well as those who will be 18 during the next year. The register is published locally in public libraries, etc. and it is the responsibility of each elector to check their inclusion and raise objections with the ERO.

Who can have a postal vote?

The ability to vote by post used to be confined to those who could not otherwise reach the polling station. Since 2001, however, it is available on demand in Great Britain, by application to the local Returning Officer. In Northern Ireland it is still necessary to provide a valid reason, such as illness or employment, to obtain a postal vote. British citizens living abroad can register to vote for up to 15 years after living in the UK. They may vote by post or proxy.

Is voting compulsory?

No, unlike in some other countries such as Australia, voting in the United Kingdom is completely optional. You do not have to vote, although you do have to register.

I want to see a particular party in Government but don't like my local candidate. What can I do?

Unfortunately there is no easy answer to this question. You only have one vote to use as you wish and must decide which is the most important factor for you. Remember your involvement in decision making does not have to end with your vote. You can lobby your MP over issues that you feel strongly about and can support pressure groups to try to bring about change. Your vote will give you a package of measures: support the areas that you approve of and try to secure change in areas where you disagree.

Constituencies

What is a constituency?

The United Kingdom is divided up into areas known as constituencies. You live in a constituency and will register to vote there. Each party contesting a constituency (seat) will select one prospective candidate to be the MP. There may also be independent candidates. You have one vote that you cast for the person who you wish to represent you in Parliament. Through this you also vote for the party which you wish to be in Government.

How many constituencies are there?

There are currently 646 constituencies: 529 in England, 59 in Scotland, 40 in Wales and 18 in Northern Ireland. The average size of a constituency electorate is approximately 68,500. More rural constituencies are known as 'county constituencies' and more urban constituencies are known as 'borough constituencies'.

How are constituencies determined?

Constituency boundaries are determined by a number of factors: geographical features, local government boundaries, area and population. Under the Parliamentary Constituencies Act 1986 constituencies are kept under review by four permanent Boundary Commissions, one each for England, Scotland, Wales and Northern Ireland. They make reports at regular

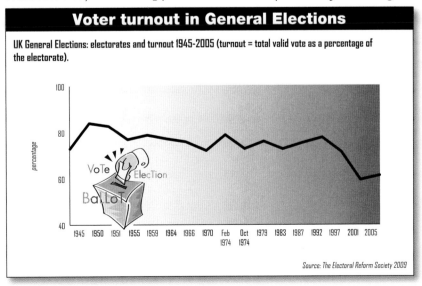

Voter turnout in General Elections

UK General Elections: electorates and turnout 1945-2005 (turnout = total valid vote as a percentage of the electorate).

Source: The Electoral Reform Society 2009

intervals recommending any changes necessary due to population change or alterations in local government boundaries. In 2005 the constituency with the largest electorate was the Isle of Wight (108,253), which is an island not easily divided. The constituency with the smallest electorate was the Na h-Eileanan an Iar (21,346), where geographical isolation is a major factor.

Following Scottish Devolution the number of constituencies in Scotland was reduced from 72 to 59 in time for the 2005 general election, bringing the number of electors per seat closer to the figure for England.

Polling day
What happens on polling day?
Each constituency is divided into a number of polling districts, each of which has a polling station. Most polling stations are in public buildings such as schools, town halls or council offices, but other buildings can be used on request. Voting takes place on election day from 07.00-22.00 in each constituency. Voters are sent a polling card in advance, but it is not compulsory to take this to the polling station. Only those voters whose names appear on the electoral register are eligible to vote.

Voting is by secret ballot, and the only people allowed in the polling station are the presiding officer (who is in charge), the polling clerks, the duty police officers, the candidates, their election agents and polling agents and the voters. Just before the poll opens, the presiding officer shows the ballot boxes to those at the polling station to prove that they are empty. The boxes are then locked and sealed. In the polling station voters are directed to the presiding officer or poll clerk, who asks the voter his or her name, checks that it is on the register, and places a mark against the register entry. This records that the voter has received a ballot paper but does not show which one. The ballot papers are printed in books with counterfoils; serial numbers are printed on the back of each paper and each counterfoil. The officer or clerk also writes the voter's number on the counterfoil of the ballot paper and gives it an official mark before handing the paper to the voter. The official mark is intended to show that

the papers placed in the ballot box are genuine.

The ballot paper lists the names of the candidates in alphabetical order. Candidates of registered political parties may include their party name and emblem but other candidates can only be described as independent. Voting takes place in a booth, which is screened to maintain secrecy. The voter marks the ballot paper with a cross in the box opposite the name of the candidate of his or her choice, and folds the paper to conceal the vote before placing it in the ballot box.

A paper that is spoiled by mistake must be returned to the presiding officer. If the presiding officer is satisfied that the spoiling was accidental, another paper is provided and the first cancelled. At the end of the voting the presiding officer delivers these spoilt papers to the returning officer. The ballot boxes are then sealed and delivered to the central point, usually a public building such as a town hall, where the count is to take place.

What happens at the count?
All ballot boxes are taken to a central place in each constituency such as a town hall where counting takes place. Each ballot box is emptied, the papers mixed up and the votes counted by teams of helpers. This is done in the presence of the candidates. When all the votes have been counted the results are announced by the Returning Officer. Depending on the time it takes to bring all of the ballot boxes to the count, the final result may be announced before midnight. Most results will come in during the early hours of the morning, but some will not be known until well into the next day.

What happens if two candidates have the same number of votes?
If the result is close then either candidate can demand a recount. The Returning Officer will advise the candidates of the figures and sanction a recount. Recounts can continue until both candidates and the Returning Officer are satisfied with the result. The largest number of recounts ever held is seven, recorded on several occasions.

If, after recounts, both candidates have exactly the same number of votes, then the result is decided by lot. This is

done by the Returning Officer. Since universal suffrage in 1918 this has not been necessary: the smallest majority recorded is two votes, gained by the then Labour candidate for Ilkeston, A. J. Flint, in 1931, and again by the Liberal Democrat MP for Winchester, Mark Oaten, in May 1997.

The electoral system
Which electoral system do we use?
The electoral system used in the United Kingdom for elections to the House of Commons is the single member constituency with simple majority, also known as the first-past-the-post system.

What does this actually mean?
As has been explained, the country is divided up into single constituencies. Each party wishing to contest the constituency (seat) offers one candidate or representative. Each voter has one vote that he or she casts for the party or representative of his or her choice. The candidate with the largest number of votes is elected to be the Member of Parliament for that constituency. So, for example, in the example below Candidate A, who received 20,000 votes, would be elected even though 25,000 votes (56% of the total) went against him/her. The party which gains the most seats in the House of Commons then forms the Government.

What are the advantages of this system?
The first-past-the-post system is relatively simple and easy to understand. It is inexpensive to operate and produces a result fairly quickly. Each constituency elects one representative who can identify with his or her area. Constituents know whom to approach when they have a problem. One party generally gains a majority in the House of Commons so voters know what to expect and which policies will be carried out.

Are there any disadvantages to this system?
1 Since the candidate who wins has only to secure a simple majority – more votes than his or her nearest rival – more people in total may have voted for other candidates than for him or her.
2 A party which comes consistently

second or third in constituencies but wins very few outright can obtain a sizeable proportion of the votes, but few seats. This is a problem faced particularly by the Liberal Democrats. For example, in 1992 they received 17.8% of the votes cast, but won only 3.1% of the seats.

3 It is possible for the party that forms the Government to have received fewer votes than its nearest rival.

4 The total electorate of constituencies varies for a number of reasons, including geographical considerations – thus the winner in a smaller constituency can have fewer votes than the runner-up in a larger constituency.

5 A number of seats are considered 'safe' – one party generally wins. Voters who do not support this party may feel that there is no point in voting at all.

Are there any alternative systems?
There are a number of possible alternatives to the first-past-the-post system. Most of these are designed to make the result, in terms of seats won, more proportional to the distribution of votes cast. For example, the Additional Member System is used for elections to the Scottish Parliament, the National Assembly for Wales, and the Greater London Assembly. Each elector has two votes, the first for a constituency member and the second for a party list. The

allocation of additional members from the list serves to correct the disproportionality arising from the election of constituency members. The Single Transferable Vote is used for elections to the Northern Ireland Assembly. Voters are able to rank as many candidates as they wish in order of preference, and those candidates who reach a certain quota are deemed to have been elected. The surplus votes of candidates are distributed on the basis of preferences to the remaining candidates. The European Parliament is elected on the basis of a list system. The UK is divided into regions and the elector selects the party that he or she wishes to represent that region; the party creates a list of candidates for the region and fills the seats it wins from that list. There is no opportunity for the ordinary elector to express a preference for an individual candidate.

The candidate for whom I voted was not elected, so who will represent me?
Once elected, your Member of Parliament is the representative of everyone in his or her constituency, regardless of whether they voted or not. Your MP will not ask, nor expect to be told, which way you voted and will seek to help all constituents in the same way.

How can I communicate with my Member of Parliament?
If you want your MP to represent your views then it is important that you communicate with him or her. You may see your MP in your constituency at local functions, openings, etc. He or she will probably visit places such as schools and factories and may even meet people in busy places such as shopping centres.

You can write to your MP either in your constituency or at the House of Commons, London SW1A 0AA. Many MPs also have e-mail addresses.

You can lobby your MP in Westminster at any time when the House of Commons is in session. It is always sensible to make an appointment first, as your MP may be too busy to see you or may be elsewhere.

Most MPs hold constituency surgeries or advice bureaux where constituents can express their views or discuss their problems. Details of when and where your MP will be holding surgeries are usually published in local

papers and in such places as public libraries. Sometimes appointments need to be made, but there are often times when you can turn up and wait.

By-elections

A by-election occurs when a Member dies, retires or is disqualified from membership of the House of Commons. Voting takes place only in the constituency without a Member. If there are several vacant seats then a number of by-elections can be held on the same day. If a vacancy occurs when the House is in session then the Motion for a new Writ of election is customarily moved by the Chief Whip of the party that formerly held the seat. There is no time limit within which a new Writ has to be issued following the vacancy occurring, although by convention it is usually done within three months. The sitting party will obviously seek to choose a time when they hope to win. There have been instances of seats remaining vacant longer than six months before a by-election and seats are sometimes left vacant towards the end of a Parliament, to be filled by the subsequent general election.

How often do by-elections take place?
It is impossible to predict when a by-election will occur. There were a total of 31 by-elections in the 1983-87 Parliament with 15 being held on 23 January 1986 after the resignation on 17 December 1985 of all 15 MPs representing constituencies in Northern Ireland. Only 15 by-elections occurred in the 1997-2001 Parliament and six in the 2001-2005 Parliament.

What happens in the time before a by-election when there is no MP?
While a vacancy exists, constituency matters are handled by a Member of the same party in a neighbouring constituency. When a new Member has been elected all outstanding matters are handled by him or her.

⇨ The above information is reprinted with kind permission from UK Parliament. Visit www.parliament.uk for more information.
© Crown copyright

Election jargon buster

Information from Y-Vote MockElections

Ballot paper

This is the piece of paper you use to make your vote. It shows a list of candidates and voters have to write a cross next to their choice.

Candidate

A person who wants to be elected or has been nominated to be elected is called a candidate.

Canvasser

People who want a candidate to win can help them by becoming a canvasser for their election campaign. A canvasser asks voters who they will vote for and tries to get as many people as possible to vote for their candidate.

Constituency

The UK is divided up into 646 areas called constituencies. The voters in each constituency get to elect one MP to represent the people in their area.

Election campaign

Around election time, candidates and their supporters organise events and activities to convince people that they are the best person to vote for.

Electoral register

Across the UK there are electoral registers: these are lists of all the people who have decided they want to vote at elections. You must have your name on this list before you can vote.

Electorate

This is what we call everyone who is able to vote in an election.

Manifesto

This is something that political parties write around the time of an election, which tells us what they would do if the got elected. A manifesto usually contains pledges (plans of action) on important issues and is often a big part of the election campaign.

MP

At a general election, the people in a constituency (area) can vote to decide who will represent them in Parliament. The person they choose is called a Member of Parliament or an MP.

Parliament

Where new laws are debated and created.

Poll card

This card is sent to everybody who is registered to vote – it has important information about the election like when, where and what time to vote.

Press officer

Press officers work for a candidate or a political party and their job is to tell people working in the media about the candidate's good qualities. Press officers want to get good things about their candidate into the newspapers or on to radio and television.

Spin doctor

Spin doctors help show their candidate in the best light by organising events like photo opportunities with local people.

⇨ The above information is re-printed with kind permission from Y-Vote MockElections. Visit www.mockelections.co.uk for more.

© Hansard Society

Tackling voter disengagement

Information from the Electoral Reform Society

Aside from cheating and compulsion, turnout can be raised only by making voting easier or more attractive. This can be done with large-scale schemes affecting the way votes are cast, such as postal voting or e-voting, or with smaller initiatives affecting elections as a whole.

Making voting easier

Providing a choice of polling stations

One way of making voting easier is to increase the number of places where it is possible to cast one's vote. Allowing

people to vote in places like shopping centres has already been trialled, although only for 'early voting', i.e. voting before polling day.

But now that electoral registers are held electronically, it should be quite possible to allow electors to vote anywhere they want in the local authority area on the day of the election. If all polling stations had an online connection to the central register, an elector could vote at any polling station – for example at a bus or railway station on the way to work, at a shopping centre, or in a polling station outside the elector's own polling district – and that a vote had been cast would be recorded on the computerised register, preventing the elector from voting more than once.

The costs and benefits of such

a scheme are, however, unclear, as is it difficult to estimate how many more people it would encourage to vote, how much extra it would cost to administer, and how secure the system would be.

Weekend voting

An oft-voiced recommendation to raise the number of people going to the ballot box in Britain is to move polling day from Thursday to the weekend (a whole weekend would be needed to accommodate people with religious objections to voting on either Saturday or Sunday).

Aside from cheating and compulsion, turnout can be raised only by making voting easier or more attractive

---

The argument is obvious enough. People work long hours, or have long commutes that disincentivise going to a polling station. A weekend would give more people more time to vote, and at a time when they would likely be less tired and more amenable to the idea of a little walk.

Despite this logic, evidence that weekend voting increases turnout is scanty. Countries voting at weekends have been found to have higher turnouts, but countries that have moved polling day have seen no rise in turnout.

Weekend voting has been piloted in local elections, but owing to poor publicity, and confusion caused by the rest of the country voting on a Thursday, the trials were not particularly helpful. The Electoral Commission has recommended that further trials should take place. To avoid national and local publicity working in different directions, testing weekend voting at by-elections would seem a sensible way forward.

Weekend voting remains at best only a minor step towards higher turnout and engagement. Just as work may discourage people from voting on a Thursday, families, holidays and hangovers may discourage voting on a weekend. When weekend voting was piloted in Watford in 2000, a relatively low proportion of younger voters turned up.

There is a stronger case for a move to weekend voting in European Parliament elections, as at present votes cast on a Thursday cannot be counted until voting takes place in most other EU countries. Weekend voting would allow the votes to be counted immediately after the close of polls, which would seem a much more sensible arrangement.

Making voting more attractive

Making election day a public holiday

Elections in Britain are fairly mundane affairs. Our political culture may not be so drawn to the Hollywood razzmatazz and plutocratic placard-waving of American elections, but

even so, elections in the UK can sometimes seem like little more than a side-show that fewer and fewer people find interesting.

There is, therefore, a lot to be said for jazzing the whole occasion up, and giving everyone the day off to celebrate the democratic process.

A 'None of the Above' option on the ballot

It has often been suggested that people would be more likely to turn up to vote if they had the choice of voting for no one. Amid the debate about compulsory voting, there are many that believe a 'None of the Above' (NOTA) option should be as compulsory to the ballot paper as turning out is for the voter.

However, others believe that a NOTA box on the ballot paper encourages abstention, and that if people want to cast an invalid vote, it's not too hard to work it out for themselves.

It is also questionable how much more attractive elections would be if NOTA were a listed option on the ballot paper. It may win plaudits in pre-election chit-chat, but how many people are really likely to be roused from whatever else they were doing to trudge along to a polling station just to express their disapproval of all that was on offer?

⇨ The above information is reprinted with kind permission from the Electoral Reform Society. Visit www. electoral-reform.org.uk for more information.

© Electoral Reform Society

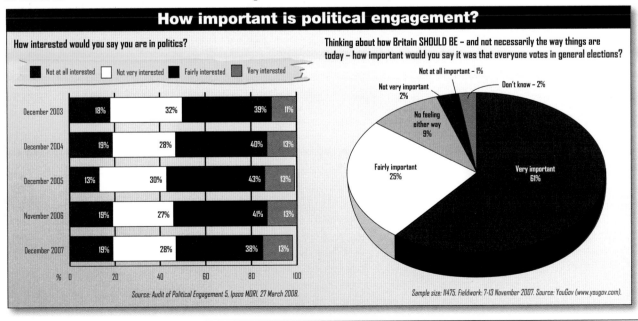

How important is political engagement?

How interested would you say you are in politics?

	Not at all interested	Not very interested	Fairly interested	Very interested
December 2003	18%	32%	39%	11%
December 2004	19%	28%	40%	13%
December 2005	13%	30%	43%	13%
November 2006	19%	27%	41%	13%
December 2007	19%	28%	38%	13%

Source: Audit of Political Engagement 5. Ipsos MORI, 27 March 2008.

Thinking about how Britain SHOULD BE – and not necessarily the way things are today – how important would you say it was that everyone votes in general elections?

Not at all important – 1%
Don't know – 2%
Not very important 2%
No feeling either way 9%
Fairly important 25%
Very important 61%

Sample size: 11475. Fieldwork: 7-13 November 2007. Source: YouGov (www.yougov.com).

Compulsory voting

Information from the Electoral Reform Society

Perhaps the most obvious way in which political disengagement is measured is through turnout figures. Thanks to its overt nature and ability to generate headlines, low turnout is a problem. One of the solutions to this problem is the fairly self-explanatory idea of compulsory voting.

Given that ballots are cast secretly, compulsory voting is not actually compulsory voting, but compulsory ballot casting, which is a little different. Leaving aside the semantics for now though, the basic idea of compulsory voting is that failure to turn up to a polling station on election day should be made illegal and met with a punishment, which, depending on where one lives, can range from a small fine to the threat of imprisonment (although there are no known cases of incarceration resulting directly from not voting).

Arguments used in support of compulsory voting

⇨ By raising turnout, compulsory voting can make the governing party or coalition appear more legitimate, as its power is very likely to be based on the support of a greater proportion of the population.

⇨ Forcing people to vote has an educative effect, along the lines of 'if you're going to do something, you might as well do it properly'. The idea is that once compelled, people will make more of an effort to cast an informed vote.

⇨ It is everyone's duty to vote, to make sure that a government works effectively. Compulsion ensures that this responsibility isn't shirked.

⇨ Making everyone vote reduces the effect of random factors on the result, like poor transport, poor weather.

⇨ Compulsion leaves parties free to campaign on policies, rather than utilising resources on 'getting out the vote'. This also, to some extent, reduces the role of money in elections. It is also sometimes argued that this leads to a drop in negative campaigning, as there is little to be gained from tactics aimed purely at persuading opposition voters to stay at home.

⇨ High levels of participation in voting may encourage higher levels of participation in other forms of political life.

⇨ Compulsory voting can enhance a sense of community, as everyone is in it together. This can be especially helpful in bringing new people in to community life. It also counteracts the vicious cycle of social exclusion where those that don't vote end up without any policies geared towards them, further discouraging them from getting involved.

Arguments used against compulsory voting

⇨ It is a limit on freedom. The right to vote contains the right not to vote, to be apolitical. Even the safeguard of a chance to abstain infringes on one's right to sit around doing nothing.

⇨ A higher voter turnout cannot be said to heighten the legitimacy of a government when the voters have been forced into giving their support. If the will of the voters is, *ceteris paribus*, to stay at home, it has a right to be reflected.

⇨ Compulsory voting merely hides the problem, rather than solving it. By hiding the problem, it allows parliament to ignore more important measures that would do something to tackle the root causes of voter disengagement.

⇨ Those that don't like being told what to do will be disproportionately inclined to vote against the people making them go out to vote, i.e. the government. This isn't such a problem, however, as incumbency has enough advantages of its own.

⇨ Compulsory voting encourages 'donkey voting', i.e. simply voting for anyone to get it out of the way. This also biases the vote in favour of the top candidate on the ballot. It is estimated that 'donkey voting' accounts for about one per cent of all votes cast in a compulsory system.

⇨ By removing incentives for political parties to mobilise their support, compulsory voting favours established parties over minor parties and independents, whose supporters tend to be more inherently motivated.

⇨ With regards to the United Kingdom, it would be especially tough to implement, as it would be seen as a quick fix that had partisan consequences, and an awful lot of people (estimates suggest over five million) would not co-operate.

Real world evidence of compulsory voting

There are many countries around the world that use compulsory voting, either in whole or in part. A list of them can be found by scanning the CIA World Factbook. Some countries, such as Venezuela and the Netherlands, used to have compulsory voting, but have since abolished it.

The exact nature of compulsory voting, where practised, differs around the world. A few examples are briefly investigated below:

Belgium

Compulsory voting has existed in Belgium since 1892. Entering a polling booth is mandatory, but marking a ballot paper is not. After the election, a list of all non-attendees is sent to the office of the public prosecutor.

Prosecutions are carried out where there is an absence of a decent excuse. Explanations such as a medically certified illness, being abroad or an 'act of God' are usually good enough reasons to escape without punishment.

Punishments work on an upward scale. A first offence receives a small fine, which can rise for repeat offenders. Continued non-attendance can result in the offender being barred from the electoral list for 10 years, making them ineligible for a nomination, distinction or promotion by a public authority.

Australia

Voting has been compulsory in Australia since 1924. Like Belgium, once at the polling station, there is no obligation to complete a ballot paper.

Also like Belgium, a good excuse circumnavigates a punishment.

The set fine for non-attendance is $A20 (under £10). About five per cent of non-voters pay this straight away, with almost everyone else providing a valid reason for not voting. A few people take their case to court, where, if they lose, the fine rises to $A50 plus costs. Refusal to pay this can result in community service or a couple of days in jail.

Brazil and Ecuador

In Brazil, voting is only compulsory if you're aged between 18 and 70 and literate. Voting for illiterates, 16- and 17-year-olds and those over 70 is voluntary.

Similarly, in Ecuador, voting is compulsory except for those over 65 and illiterates, for whom it is optional.

Punishments

Although in Greece, it is technically possible to go to prison for not voting, no one ever has and it is highly unlikely anyone ever will. Global punishments for non-attendance on election day tend to be rather benign.

Indeed, in many countries, compulsory voting law isn't enforced at all; the hope is that the mere existence of the law is enough to spur people into turning out, without having to worry about chasing down the rebels later on. The law exists more to strengthen the idea of civic responsibility than to force people to go and vote. In many places, this works, although not as effectively as where the law is more strictly enforced.

In Austria, for example, voting is compulsory in only two regions and despite both having weak sanctions, turnout is higher than the national average.

The most common punishment for non-compliance is a simple fine. However, there are other ways in which non-voters can lose out.

In Belgium, it is possible to become disenfranchised (this takes at least four elections and 15 years of not voting). In Peru, voters get a stamped voting card to carry around for months after the election to prove that they have voted. This card is required to obtain certain goods and services from some public offices.

A similar scheme is run in Bolivia, with people who can't prove that they voted left unable to claim their salary from the bank for three months after the election.

There are a range of other, less formal, inconveniences for non-voters, like not being able to get a job in Belgium's public sector, trouble getting a new passport or driving licence in Greece. In Italy, non-voters used to be 'named and shamed' in a list posted outside the local town hall, although this rarely happens now.

Compulsory voting and a 'None of the Above' option

Some argue that there should be a box on the ballot paper to register an official abstention, particularly if voting is compulsory. It is argued that this is a reasonable concession to offer the reluctant voter, and a Bill arguing for compulsory voting presented to Parliament in 2001 by Gareth Thomas had this provision. However, by placing such a box on a ballot paper the electoral system would draw attention to the 'None of the Above' option and encourage it. The point of compulsory voting is to reverse the burden of effort and expectation from abstaining to voting, and to add an abstention box rather goes against this purpose. It is not unreasonable to expect someone intending to cast an invalid vote to figure it out for themselves.

The Electoral Commission's conclusion

In 2003, the Electoral Commission took a quick look at the issue of compulsory voting. They concluded that:

The Electoral Commission recognises that compulsory voting would not in itself address the underlying causes of low turnout, and in particular the apparent lack of engagement between potential voters and politics. However, the Commission believes there is merit in opening up the question of compulsory voting for wider debate, and that it should be examined in more detail as one of a series of options which might help to contribute to higher rates of participation in elections. The Commission will be conducting research into international use of compulsory voting as a first step.

⇨ The above information is reprinted with kind permission from the Electoral Reform Society. Visit www.electoral-reform.org.uk for more information.

© Electoral Reform Society

A sure way to get 100% voter turnout... pass a law that forces politicians to keep their election pledges.

Or else end up in jail!

Are young people allergic to politics?

An extract from a survey by the Hansard Society via their HeadsUp forum on behalf of the Youth Citizenship Commission

Introduction

The Youth Citizenship Commission was set up to look at ways of developing young people's understanding of citizenship and increasing their participation in politics. The Commissioners were tasked with finding out what citizenship means to young people, whether they think they should be able to vote at 16 and how our political system can best listen and respond to their concerns. They used the HeadsUp forum to find out what young people up and down the country think about these issues. The Commission will report back to the Prime Minister in late spring 2009 and the opinions of HeadsUp users will be included in their findings. There will be an opportunity for HeadsUp users to find out more in a debate (15 June-3 July 2009) that will discuss the findings once the final report has been written.

There were 394 posts made in the forum from 171 HeadsUp users. This forum was the most popular yet in terms of the number of contributions it received. The discussions on the forum were broad but the general themes and directions of the debate are highlighted below along with all the practical suggestions given by forum users.

Politics

HeadsUp users overwhelmingly said that they found politics boring and too complicated. The use of technical terms and long words account for much of this negative feeling.

There are a lot of words used in politics that makes no sense to us watsoever, they need to get of their high horse and come down to the level that we can understand.

i think the bit about using difficult language

is true its one of politicians' weapons of keeping the public out of their business.

The image of Parliament as portrayed in the media emphasised how young people felt politics wasn't for them.

There were many comments that emphasised the connection between politics being relevant (or irrelevant) to young people and their subsequent interest in politics. There was a lot of disagreement about the extent to which politics affects young people, how far up young people's issues are on the political agenda, and therefore whether there was any point being interested or involved. Most of the comments below show a resemblance with the opinions of the electorate at large – young people made it clear that they wouldn't get involved if the issues didn't affect them or they didn't think they had a chance of influencing the outcome.

Laws do involve us young people. For example, the 10p tax on basic essentials. My favourite chocolate 'chomp' was 10p years ago however...it is annoying that there has been a rise 0f 5p, just like Haribos have been increased to 15p. This is due to Alistair Darling who did not seem to think about young people when making the law.

It's not that we're not interested it just doesn't directly affect us. A rise in tax, yes we know that sounds bad and yes we know our parents, etc. are going to moan about it but unless you actually pay taxes then you sort of just accept it.

We think that it only affect adults. the thing is that young people find politics boring and not interesting enough, we do not see anything significant enough about the laws of today.. because it doesnt feel like it is working.

As is mentioned above, a major part of being interested in politics was connected to the ability of young people to effect change or for their ideas to have an outcome. Changing the voting age to 16 was supported by a majority of 3:1 in the forum. Most young people felt that politics might be worthwhile getting involved in and might affect them more if they could vote.

I think the main reason that us teenagers dont really like politics is because of the voting age. when you cant vote you felt left... it really should be reduced to 16.

The language they use makes it boring. I think they dont aim it at us because we can't vote so to them out opinion dosn't matter. It doesnt effect them if we don't want them to run our country, as long as they have the older generation on their side they will still get votes. They should let us vote at a younger age, if we got to vote at the age of 16 would have our say. At the moment are views don't really count.

i just think that we are a bit fustrated because we don't get a say in what our country is like. If young people had a chance to have their say then maybe they would start to like polotics a bit more.

Those that were against votes at 16 thought that either 16-year-olds would not have made up their minds sufficiently about politics or were not well-informed enough to be trusted with a vote.

I know that if I carry on as ignorant as I am about poltics on both a local and national level then when I turn 18 I won't have a clue who to vote for. I don't think that lowering the voting age will be sucessful because 16 year olds are still trying to work out what they believe.

Politics in general suffered from an

image problem and a misunderstanding of what it involves. The main thing associated with the word politics was old men in suits shouting at each other in Parliament. Issues that were important to young people were not seen as being 'political'.

When I think of politics, I see a group of men debating about one thing or another, and after hours of endless droning, nothing is solved. However, I am sensible enough to recognise that it is more than that, but what exactly?...I am keen on debating and campaigning, and finding ways to help combat issues in today's rickety world, but how is the question, as well as the fact that, what is it to do with politics?

Young people's mayors were also discussed as a way young people can already get involved in decisions and voting in their local areas. They were seen positively but some were dubious as to how many voted in these elections and how widely publicised they were.

You say that a young mayor is in every borough..but how many of us young people actually know about this...if you say so can you give me the statistics of how many people voted.

A lack of knowledge about how to get involved in projects and initiatives that currently exist was a consistent theme of the forum.

Politicians

Politicians drew many criticisms from young people for being out of touch, not listening, not speaking simply enough, setting a bad example, not visiting young people and blaming them for all society's ills!

It is believed politicians do not pay attention to us young people. They look down on us and point the finger at us whenever something is going wrong in the comuunity. Politicians should walk with us and involve us someway

After watching one session of PMQs a couple of weeks ago I actually felt quite embarrassed at the way Cameron and Brown had descended into scoring 'points' of each other rather than focusing on the real issues... Politicians should be setting an example to young people, not trading personal insults while avoiding actually answering questions.

Maybe politicians should get around more – like doing extra sports like imagine Gordon brown doin the marathon

Young people felt that politicians also needed to be more representative of the population as a whole in order to appeal to voters and young people.

I think that polititions give away a negative imgage towards childeren beause they are usually old and crusty. Maybe if a young, interesting, fun politition was to come by then it would appeal to kids.

i belive young people are rather fed up with the politics sorounding them than a lack of interest becuase recently we saw a vast number of young involved in the US presidential election. So i think we need a change in our male dominate and instituionally racist Britian.

In terms of how they would like to be contacted by politicians, young people overall were keen on their MPs being on MySpace or Bebo. A majority of 2:1 said they thought it was a good idea. They felt that this would give them a better understanding of what their politicians were like and would allow them to stay in contact more effectively.

I do think that our MP should be on myspace because, many young people use it and if an MP does, it would show that he is with the trends and is able to comunicate with young people in a way that they would actually listen... children may also start to think differently about MPs' and politics, they may start to think that they are not all boring poeple who do not understand kids and start thinking that they can be child friendly. Children respect and listen to them more.

I think that MP's and politicans don't take the time to talk to young people. They ask for the opinions of adults and don't really take into consideration what we want. I think if MP's and politicians were on facebook or myspace then they would be able to hear what the youth want and would be able to communicate with them in a better way.

However there were also those that felt MPs on social networking sites could be a little embarrassing or might be invading young people's space (although usually social networking sites do require consent from users before any contact is made).

I don't think that MP's on MySpace etc will work at all, politicians seem so desperate to be 'down with the kids' and thought of as 'cool' and representative of today's youth rather than concerned with the actual issues

that affect them. I would rather vote for someone who will fight for our rights and support our issues rather than someone who can speak in slang and write in text type on facebook.

There was also support for politicians leaving Westminster and coming to where young people are to explain how politics works or to update them with what they are currently doing to improve the local area.

Children are put off by politics because all you ever see on the news is old people talking in the House of Lords of The House of Commons. Politictians should go into school or youth centres and talk about what they want in their local area. They should make it less formal and talk about that matters which affect everyday children.

Media and information

The media was widely blamed by young people for making Parliament and politics seem much more complicated than it needed to be. It was also criticised for its negative portrayal of young people and politicians.

I think There Should Be More Press On The Good Things Goverment Do Because i find The Mistakes Or Bad Remarks Are High-lighted In Our Local Papers And Our Favourite Television Chanels.

Most teenagers only know about politicians mentioned in the news and media and not about everyone else that is in involved in making decisions. It's not all about one single politician

When it comes to young people they dont understand the current worlds circumstances they just think its the lack of role models but think about it who is our role model its the government!! and we all know that because we hear about it more in the current news than anywhere else and if we keep on hearing criticism we will think they are not doing anything about the crisis in the world eg. the bombings in india. or the credit crunch.

They almost universally complained about the lack of clear, simple information available for young people and this exacerbated the idea that politics wasn't for them or that adults were purposefully excluding them from politics. HeadsUp users had plenty of ideas about how they would like to be more informed or learn about politics. TV seemed to be the most favoured medium and many were keen on seeing more political debates on TV that involved politicians and celebrities.

I think that the politics is useful and if we had a children's politician group programme that celebrites hosted then more children will be interested in the subject

Advertising politics to young people and how important it is was also highlighted by many of users in the forum.

To get teenagers more interested in politics I think it should be advertised like everything else. Bring it to everyone's attention how important politics is and how is affects EVERYONE, so we all might as well have our say. There should be more sites like this [HeadsUp], TV shows too.

Citizenship lessons

There appeared to be little awareness that citizenship was compulsory in secondary schools or that it was linked to politics, as more political education was one of the solutions regularly suggested by young people to combat apathy or ignorance.

If there were lessons in Citizenship based specifically on politics, it would increase our understanding of it.

How politically engaged are the UK's young citizens?

Citizenship is a GSCE option in which children can learn more about politics, however, this is optional and I don't think that enough is being done to teach people about it from a younger age than a GCSE level...This option is just encouraging people who already are interested in politics, not educating the people who are naive about it.

More in-depth citizenship lessons that were explicitly related to politics were suggested to increase young people's knowledge.

Defining citizenship

HeadsUp users were less likely to see citizenship as something given to everyone as a right and more in terms of the duties citizenship entails to wider society. This was evident in their definitions of being a good citizen as not breaking the law, being environmentally friendly and helping others wherever possible. The feeling of community, attachment to their local area and all citizens being linked through citizenship was particularly strong.

A citizen means that you are united with everyone else in your neighbourhood and you be friendly with each other it also means to abide by the laws that the government passes and that you should not be a criminal as this breaks down communities

A good citizen is someone who does things like: recycle, not litter, helps the community, etc...I think a bad citizen is someone who does the complete opposite. Also i feel that being a citizen means that you are leagally here and a part of your country or city.

Equality, respect and a multi-cultural society without discrimination were also seen as synonymous with British citizenship.

Citizenship in Britain has changed over the years as more and more people have moved here. I think it means that no matter what your race, beliefs or culture is you are still a part of the country and no one should tell you otherwise because of your differences.

To me a citizen is someone who do doesnt descriminate others and can live together in harmony.

Volunteering

Volunteering was almost universally seen as a good thing by HeadsUp users but there seemed to be little knowledge of the diversity of volunteering opportunities. Most users seemed to think the only options for them would be working in a charity shop or picking up litter.

The only holdback is that the kind of volenteer work around, isn't really interesting to most people. They think that working in shops and picking up litter is boring. In a way I have to agree with them; that there aren't that many choices to pick from.

Better advertising for projects was highlighted as a good way to encourage more young people to volunteer.

There are not many advertisements that aim there charity work at the youth. I believe that if there was more out there for us then we'd be more likely to get involved.

Volunteering projects in schools, perhaps coordinated by the local council, were suggested as a way of giving pupils a place to find volunteer projects.

I can do volunteer work through school and I think most of the students do get involved. But this is becasue there is a teacher who makes the initial link for us and the school/care home/charity. perhaps if there were youth volunteering groups put in place in schools either by the local councils or by a teacher then students would feel as though they could get involved.

Many also wanted to volunteer in their local area and help with specific problems they had noticed in their community but again were unsure about how to go about this.

I did some work for a charity last week and found it much more rewarding because I had noticed that they needed help myself and done something about it.

I would like to see young people being able to volunteer in nursing homes as I have a Nan in one, and I would like to help everyone that is there not just her. I would also quite like to be able to do so with friends, it would be quite nice bonding and we'd also be helping our community. I also think it's sad that some poeple that stay in nursing homes don't get many visitors.

Those that did volunteer said they gained useful skills and did not like young people being stereotyped as lazy because it's not true of all teenagers.

I think that young people are totally under rated. for example i am part of a guide group and we do loads like fund raising for the indian children and also we sing at christmas for the elderly at a hotel.

Volunteering gives you lots of experience and helps you work well with other people. It is a good life skill to have.

⇨ Information from the Hansard Society. Visit www.hansardsociety.org.uk for more information.
© Hansard Society

Political outsiders?

Guides call for new politics for the next generation

Girls say domestic violence, gangs and knife crime, bullying and workplace equality are the most important political issues for young women today.

Girls call for a new Youth Green Paper to engage young women in politics:

⇨ *Ensuring every prospective candidates shortlist includes one person under 25.*

⇨ *Launching text and online voting.*

⇨ *Setting political parties compulsory work experience targets for 14- to 21-year-olds.*

New Girlguiding UK research has revealed that even among girls who are members of Girlguiding UK, traditionally some of the most active citizens in their age group, there is a deep disengagement from local and national politics, raising questions of whether there is even greater disillusionment among girls outside the organisation's membership.

The report, *Political Outsiders: We Care, But Will We Vote?* has been published in partnership with equality campaigners the Fawcett Society and youth campaigners the British Youth Council to coincide with the 80th anniversary of the Equal Franchise Act which gave women the same voting rights as men.

The research was conducted by Populus among approximately 1,000 girls who are members of Girlguiding UK aged between 14 and 25.

Girls in guiding are committed volunteers – values promoted by Girlguiding UK and its programme. 96 per cent of the girls questioned engage in volunteering, spending an average of just over two hours a week. By contrast, less than half the numbers who volunteer have any involvement with politics (45 per cent) and those who do commit significantly less time – an average of 25 minutes a week. Indeed, in interviews conducted on the basis of the findings, girls explained that they just do not see participating in politics as relevant to their role as engaged citizens. As one put it: 'When I think about being an active citizen, I don't think about politics. I volunteer – but politics just never occurred to me.'

A third of girls also believe involvement in politics is declining over time and say they are less engaged in politics than their parents' generation (34 per cent). Two-fifths feel engagement has levelled off (41 per cent).

Even among girls who are members of Girlguiding UK, traditionally some of the most active citizens in their age group, there is a deep disengagement from local and national politics

---

When it comes to barriers to political participation, over a quarter of girls are put off by insufficient information about how they should take part (27 per cent). Many are also sceptical about its impact. Around a fifth are deterred by feeling politics is not worth the effort (20 per cent) or cannot make a difference (17 per cent). In interviews, girls said that small numbers of young or female MPs also made them feel that politics was not open to them. As one explained: 'You never see your local MP and when you do – he's an old man.' Another said: 'When one of the most high-profile women in politics feels she has to resign to spend more time with her family – it makes women feel that they can't do both.'

Over half of respondents (52 per cent) named stopping domestic violence against women and children as the most important issue for young women today. Speaking out against young people and gangs who carry knives came second, named by 46 per cent, followed by standing up against bullying (39 per cent), making sure women have the same career

What's the point of getting involved when there's nothing here relevant to my life or my peers?

VOTING INFORMATION

opportunities as men (36 per cent) and combating the pressure on young women to have sex before they are ready (33 per cent). Banning models being air-brushed was named by around a quarter (27 per cent), as was fighting for equal pay (25 per cent).

On the back of the research findings, girls in guiding have developed a call to action for the Government, political parties, policy makers and the media. The Plan for Participation calls for new legislation - enshrined in a new Youth Green Paper - outlining fresh policies to engage young people. Girls advise government to recommend compulsory political education in schools, appoint a well-known Minister for Young People and recruit a panel of young ambassadors to advocate political participation. Girls call on political parties to recruit young MPs under 25 and to set annual targets for offering work experience placements to 14- to 21-year-olds.

The girls also favour new schemes to allow voting via the technology they use everyday - particularly text messages and the Internet. They would like to see young people be given greater access to politics via the media, recommending the appointment of youth correspondents by national media outlets and launching a monthly young people's political press conference. Finally, girls call for UCAS points to be awarded for active citizenship - to formalise its value among universities, employers and the world beyond.

Girlguiding UK's Chief Executive Denise King said: 'Girls in guiding are committed volunteers, who care deeply about a wide range of issues. But they are sceptical about whether politics can help make a difference. As we approach the next election, the first time many of our members will be able to vote, it is vital that everyone who cares about giving young people a voice listens carefully to their recommendations. Eight decades on from the Equal Franchise Act we all have a responsibility to get young women engaged in the decision-making processes affecting their lives - bringing positive change for them, their communities and us all.'
1 December 2008

⇨ The above information is reprinted with kind permission from Girlguiding UK. Visit www.girlguiding. org.uk for more information.
© Girlguiding UK

Got a taste for it?

There are lots of ways to get involved in democracy throughout the year, not just at election time

If you want to have your views heard on an issue you care about you could:
⇨ submit a petition;
⇨ write a letter to your local representative;
⇨ provide evidence to a committee;
⇨ get your representative to ask a question on your behalf;
⇨ get involved in a youth council or youth parliament; or
⇨ start a local campaign.

Submitting a petition
What is a petition?
A petition is a list of names and basic details of people that support a particular issue or campaign. They are normally used to draw attention to a cause. Petitions highlight the level of support for the cause locally, nationally or internationally.

You may be approached on the street and asked to sign a petition. This is a very basic way of becoming involved in the political process.

Many petitions are also distributed by email or on a website, which obviously has some practical advantages over standing on street corners!

If you are campaigning on a particular issue you may decide that you want to formally submit a petition to the UK Parliament or another democratic body. To do this you need to follow special guidelines. Here are some pointers on how to submit a formal petition to:
Your local council
Each council has different requirements so it is best to consult their website or ask your local councillor. Petitions at this level will be focused on local issues, such as calls to improve a local playground or to prevent a closure of a local facility. They can have quite a big impact at this level if there is a lot of support for your campaign.
The UK Parliament
Anyone in the UK can submit a petition to Parliament. Petitions may be sent to Parliament postage-free and can be presented formally by a Member of Parliament (MP) with a short speech, or informally in the Petition Bag which hangs on the back of the Speaker's Chair.

Petitions have a long history as members of the public have used them to make their feelings known about issues that concern them. Several thousand people often sign a petition and Parliament receives over a thousand petitions each year.

For more information visit www. parliament.uk

The National Assembly for Wales
Petitions can be presented to the Petitions Clerk or any Assembly Member (AM), in writing or in person. The petitioner will be given a receipt and an explanation of what will then happen to their petition. The petition is then checked for 'reasonableness'.

The full text and the number of signatures on the petition are then published on the Internet to inform the Assembly. The petition then goes to the appropriate Assembly Minister or committee and the petitioner will receive a written reply from them. If the petition contains an issue of major importance it can also be debated in the chamber.

For more information visit www. wales.gov.uk

The Scottish Parliament

You can submit a petition to a Scottish Parliamentary Committee either in writing or through an e-petition. The Scottish Parliament has a dedicated committee to deal with petitions from individuals, groups and organisations. If you submit a petition you may be asked to speak directly with the committee to raise your concerns.

The committee can pass your petition on to other committees of the Parliament, or to other bodies and organisations outside of Parliament for further consideration. All petitions get a written response and do not rely on a Member of the Scottish Parliament (MSP) to support or push it.

For more information visit www.scottish.parliament.uk

The Northern Ireland Assembly

Public petitions can be presented by a Member of the Legislative Assembly (MLA). An MLA may present a petition to the Speaker, normally at the beginning of a day's business. The Member will 'beg leave' to lay a petition before the House. They may then say a few words explaining on whose behalf it is presented, the number of signatures attached to it and a brief summary of the content. The Member then hands over the petition.

The Speaker then sends copies of the petition to the relevant minister and Committee Chairperson.

For more information visit www.niassembly.gov.uk

Write to or email your representatives

By writing to your representatives you are making them aware of what you think about an issue. Most representatives look at all letters and emails from the people they represent. The more people who write to a representative on a particular issue, the more they will sit up and take notice.

Before you write, find out which of your representatives is responsible for the issue you are concerned about. Make it clear in your letter or email what action you would like your representative to take.

Get your representative to ask an 'official' question

All MPs, MSPs, AMs and MLAs have the right to ask or 'table' questions to government ministers and departments. You can write to your representative and request that they ask a question addressing your concerns.

There are two main forms of questions in the UK Parliament:
⇨ questions for oral (spoken) answers; and
⇨ questions for written answers.

About 50,000 of these 'parliamentary questions' are raised each year.

In the House of Commons, oral questions are asked during an official 'Question Time' which takes place for an hour on Mondays, Tuesdays, Wednesdays and Thursdays. The different government departments answer questions according to a rota and the questions asked must relate to the responsibilities of the department concerned.

There is a limit to the number of oral questions that can be asked, but MPs can ask a larger number of written questions. Questions are usually answered in seven working days. All answers are documented in 'The Questions Book' in Hansard, which is the official parliamentary record.

This is a good way to get your views heard and to get a specific answer to what may be a complicated issue. It may take some time however. Your MP may get a lot of requests to ask questions, or the department that has to be asked may not be answering again for a while. It pays to be patient!

Give evidence to an official committee

Committees are the part of our democratic institutions that investigate issues in-depth. To do this they gather evidence and make recommendations. It is possible for you or your youth organisation to give evidence to a committee to let them know your views on the issues they are investigating.

There are a number of ways you can do this.

Committees will invite 'experts' to give 'oral' evidence. This means sitting in front of the committee members and answering their questions. For example children and young people were able to provide their views on children's rights to a UK Parliament select committee on Human Rights.

It is only possible for a limited number of people to give evidence in person so committees also ask for written evidence. This means that you can send your views in to the committee to tell them what you think about the issue they are looking into.

Some committees also run discussion forums on a website so you can make your views known online.

Most of our democratic institutions have similar arrangements for

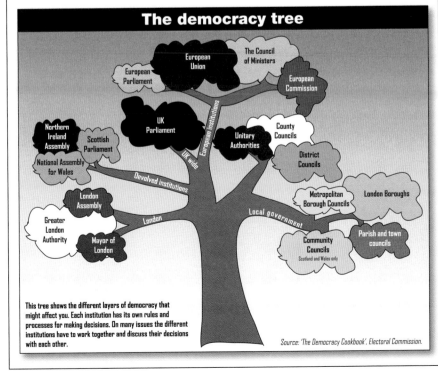

The democracy tree

This tree shows the different layers of democracy that might affect you. Each institution has its own rules and processes for making decisions. On many issues the different institutions have to work together and discuss their decisions with each other.

Source: 'The Democracy Cookbook', Electoral Commission.

giving evidence to committees and will provide guidance on how you go about doing it.

To find out what issues are currently being investigated keep an eye on the institution websites: www.parliament.uk; www.scottishparliament.uk; www.wales.gov.uk; or www.niassembly.gov.uk

Get involved in a youth forum or youth council

Your local youth forum is somewhere you can let off steam about the things that you care about. It also gives you access to the people who help make decisions about your local area. The organisations are an extension of the formal institutions of democracy and allow young people from all walks of life to come together on common issues.

Local councils are currently committed to providing opportunities for young people to put forward their views. Look out for advertisements in your local area, in your local paper or get in touch with your local authority for more details.

What is being a youth mayor all about?

Lewisham's first ever youth mayor, 17-year-old Manny Hawkes, talks about his achievements.

'I like to know what's going on around me so when I heard about the opportunity to run as youth mayor I couldn't resist. I had to get 30 young people from Lewisham to nominate me. The council then gave all the people running for youth mayor election training, which taught us how to get our ideas across clearly.

As youth mayor I'm not in charge of young people, but I advise the council on how to best serve young people in the borough. I work with a youth advisory group made up of people aged 11 to 25. We have a budget of £25,000 which we get to spend on services for young people.

Things that we've got off the ground include:

⇨ setting up a rehearsal space for bands;
⇨ running community safety workshops for young people that showed people how to develop self-awareness and deal with the fear of crime;

⇨ a directory of services – there are lots of services for young people in Lewisham, but people were unaware of what they are;
⇨ setting up the 'be involved' website – this is a direct feed into democracy where young people can access members of the council or the youth advisory group; and
⇨ running a 10 x 10 over cricket tournament for primary schools.

It's taken a while to get things happening. Working with the council requires patience because things happen slowly. You just need a bit of assertiveness and willpower. When I first started I was more laid back, but now I say 'I want this done and I want it done now!' If you can be bothered to get something done, other people will see what you do and want to get involved as well.

My advice to young people is that if you have a problem with something in your area or a problem with how the country is being run, you can't complain if you can't be bothered to do something about it. Politics affects all of us and it's not going to go away by ignoring it.'

⇨ The above information is an extract from *The Democracy Cookbook*. For more, visit the Do Politics Centre, the Electoral Commission's idea and resource hub for democracy practitioners: www.dopolitics.org.uk

© The Electoral Commission

The case for votes at 16

Information from Votes at 16

Over 1.5 million 16- and 17-year-olds are denied the vote in the United Kingdom. For years there has been a consistent demand from young people for votes at 16, and a clear case for change. That case is now overwhelming.

At 16, we can leave school, work full time and pay taxes, leave home, get married, join the armed forces, and make lots of decisions about our future.

At 16, people become adults and take control of their own futures – so why can't we have the basic right of all adult citizens of a say in how the country is run?

We're all interested in issues; from climate change to racism, from education to crime. Voting is the fundamental way that we have our say on issues, and we think that at 16, young people are mature enough to be properly listened to.

Stopping 16- and 17-year-olds from voting and having the chance to be heard sends a signal to them and to society, especially politicians, that our views aren't valid and that we aren't real citizens. At a time when people feel that politics isn't relevant to them, young people need to be encouraged to take part in democracy, not kept out from it.

Citizenship education, youth engagement campaigns and high-speed interactive media have made this generation the most politically aware and educated ever, but the number of people taking part in politics just keeps on dropping. It's time we recognised the abilities of 16-year-olds, including them in society and showing them the trust and respect that society expects of them.

It's time we gave young people the basic right of any citizen – the right to vote.

⇨ The above information is reprinted with kind permission from Votes at 16. Visit www.votesat16.org.uk for more information.

© Votes at 16

New evidence finds majority in favour of votes at 16

The Youth Citizenship Commission has today published evidence that two-thirds of respondents to its consultation back Votes at 16

The consultation ran from November 2008-January 2009, with the government-backed Commission receiving 488 responses. Of this, 66% backed lowering the voting age to 16 and the majority backed lowering the voting age to 16 in all UK elections.

Today's news demonstrates yet again the high level of support for votes at 16. The Government should listen loud and clear: Britain wants votes at 16. The time is right for voting-age reform; the time for action is now!

We want to thank everyone who put time and effort into responding. All of us should feel very pleased with the results – your input and submissions have made a real difference to the Commission's deliberations! The Commission will be releasing their final report in June this year.

The Youth Citizenship Commission is headed by Prof. Jonathan Tonge of Liverpool University, and was launched by the Government to deliver Gordon Brown's pledge to investigate the case for lowering the voting age. As well as leading the consultation on the voting age, it is examining ways of developing young people's understanding of citizenship and increasing their participation in politics.
17 April 2009

⇨ The above information is reprinted with kind permission from Votes at 16. Visit www.votesat16.org.uk for more.
© Votes at 16

Votes at 16?

By Clare Coatman

In an attempt to engage young people with the formal political process, the Youth Citizenship Commission (YCC) - a body set up this summer as part of the Governance of Britain agenda to 'examine ways of developing young people's understanding of citizenship and increase their participation in politics' - is beginning a three-month consultation on lowering the voting age to 16 – the first of a range of proposals. The consultation paper includes information on where we fit in internationally, the current legal picture (what rights and responsibilities come into effect at what ages) and the implications of both leaving the law untouched and reforming it.

16-year-olds can get married, have children and join the army. They are among those who will feel the long term impact of global warming, our foreign policy and the recent financial crisis. They will face major challenges from rising unemployment and will feel the full effects of our education policy.

On the face of it, then, it seems logical that the voting age should be lowered. However, if young people are disillusioned by and uninterested in parliamentary politics, giving them the option of voting as a lone measure can't possibly solve the deeper problem. The right 18-year-olds have to vote does not ensure a reasonable turn-out amongst that age group and, once the novelty has worn off, what would ensure reasoned and regular voting from the under-18s?

At 16 a small proportion of people are highly politically aware and active, but equally there are those who can't even name a single party or minister.

I sat through four years of compulsory Citizenship education, and my political interest and activism exists very much despite it. Like many other schools, mine rolled the lesson in with PSHCE lessons (ed – that's Personal, Social, Health and Community Education for those unfamiliar with the latest pre-16 curriculum!) leaving a vast range of content to be covered in just an hour a week. The teacher was not a specialist and was ill-prepared both for the content and for the appalling behaviour of some of the class. Many teachers do not take the subject seriously, and few students see it as anything other than an extra hour a week to chat with mates. To be at all effective more resources and creative thinking is needed. Don't just talk about community participation – get the students involved, have field trips, invite guest speakers in, have debates. Do anything other than sit in a room and plough through worksheets.

A single measure like votes at 16 won't get the job done. Citizenship education must be drastically redesigned and embedded into the wider syllabus before we have any hope of producing 16-year-olds, and adults, who are willing to engage in the political process.
21 October 2008

⇨ This article was originally published in the independent online magazine www.opendemocracy.net
© openDemocracy.net

Since citizenship education arrived

Information from the NFER (National Foundation for Educational Research)

This year marks the 10th anniversary of the first Crick report that led to the introduction of statutory citizenship education. The Citizenship Education Longitudinal Study (CELS) is tracking young people who have been experiencing citizenship education since it became statutory in schools in 2001. David Kerr from the National Foundation for Educational Research (NFER) shares the latest findings of the Study and relates them to key areas being considered by the new Youth Citizenship Commission.

This is an exciting time to be a young citizen in Britain. With citizenship issues high on the political agenda, there are increasing opportunities to learn about and experience citizenship in education. Young people are also being consulted more than ever and their opinions carry increasing influence. Chief amongst these developments is the setting up by the government of a Youth Citizenship Commission.

The Citizenship Education Longitudinal Study (CELS) began in 2001 with a cohort of over 18,000 11-year-olds and is due to make its final report in 2009/2010 when the cohort has reached 18. The main aim of CELS is to assess the short-term and long-term effects of citizenship education on students.

To date, the Study has successfully followed the cohort from age 11 to age 16 (just over 11,000 respondents left). As such, it offers the most comprehensive picture of young people's citizenship experiences, both in schools and in their communities, and how these have changed over time.

The latest CELS report focuses on young people's civic participation in and beyond school at age 16. It investigates young people's attitudes and intentions concerning formal political participation (for example,

By David Kerr, Director of the CELS Study at NFER

voting or contacting MPs) and informal civic and civil participation (including volunteering and collecting money for charity) and what influences them over time. Below is a brief review of how the latest CELS findings inform the Youth Citizenship Commission's work in relation to key themes it has been tasked to consider.

What citizenship means to young people

In terms of citizenship as civic engagement and participation:
⇨ Young people currently have a narrow conception of civic engagement and participation, limiting themselves mainly to activities such as voting and collecting money and student voice that require low levels of time, effort and commitment.
⇨ The most important factor in producing positive attitudes and strong intentions among young people about civic participation is efficacy, particularly personal efficacy – that is, a young person's belief that they can make a difference through their actions.

How to increase young people's participation in politics

In terms of their current and future participation intentions:
⇨ Young people express moderate interest in formal political participation and moderate intentions to participate in the future.
⇨ Year 11 students (age 16) are not politically apathetic but are increasingly aware of politics and of its influence, in part through increased exposure to news and current affairs.
⇨ Young people exhibit low levels of trust in politicians and political institutions, such as the European Union (EU).

- IT'S OUR RIGHT TO GET INVOLVED AND MAKE THIS A BETTER PLACE!!

SURE THEY'RE NOT JUST SAYING THAT..?

Volunteering

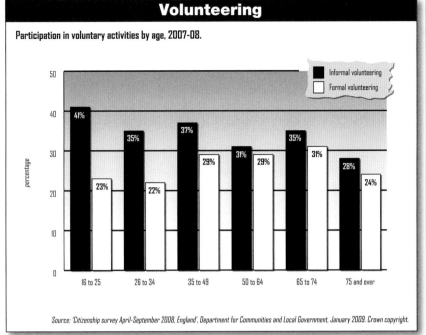

Participation in voluntary activities by age, 2007-08.

Source: 'Citizenship survey April-September 2008, England', Department for Communities and Local Government, January 2009. Crown copyright.

⇨ The majority of young people surveyed neither support a political party nor are likely to get involved in local politics nor contact politicians, such as MPs, in the future.

⇨ The projected voting levels among 16-year-old students of around 50 per cent are not sufficiently high to suggest that this cohort will vote in significantly more numbers than the cohorts immediately in front of them.

Young people currently have a narrow conception of civic engagement and participation

⇨ Young people who take an interest in news and current affairs have more positive attitudes and stronger intentions to participate in formal political processes than students with less exposure to news.

How to develop citizenship among disadvantaged groups

In terms of how background variables that influence young people's attitudes and intentions to participate:

⇨ Young people are not a homogeneous group who exhibit the same strength of attitudes and intentions.

⇨ Gender, ethnicity and socioeconomic status all combine to influence the attitudes and intentions of particular groups of students, sometimes positively and at other times less so.

⇨ Those young people with the most positive attitudes and the strongest intentions tend to be girls, those of Asian origin and those with the highest socio-economic status.

⇨ Those young people with the least positive attitudes and intentions tend to be boys, those of white British or Black origin and those with the lowest socio-economic status.

How active citizenship can be promoted through volunteering and community involvement

In terms of informal civic participation and community attachment:

⇨ Students exhibit moderate strength of intention to undertake informal civic and civil participation in the future.

⇨ 16-year-old students largely confine their informal participation to collecting money for a good cause and volunteering time to help other people, with over half of students saying they will do the former and over two-fifths the latter in the future.

⇨ Only a minority of students, around one-quarter, show any inclination to become involved in other informal activities, such as contacting a newspaper or taking part in phone-in programmes or non-violent protest.

Should the voting age be lowered to 16?

Talking recently to students in CELS case-study schools suggests a mixed response. Some are in favour, feeling that it fits with other rights and responsibilities they have at this age. However, others are opposed because some 16-year-olds are not yet mature enough and have insufficient experience to carry out so important a civic responsibility.

Key questions for the Commission

The Youth Citizenship Commission has thrown down the gauntlet of shaping the nature of citizenship in contemporary Britain. I hope that those involved in post-16 citizenship activities will use their experiences to do just that, and that this article will kick start the process. A few questions to get your learners going:

⇨ How do your experiences of and attitudes to citizenship compare with those young people (now age 16) involved in CELS?

⇨ What does citizenship mean to you, and your peers?

⇨ What is the voice of post-16 citizenship?

⇨ How should the Youth Citizenship Commission address post-16 citizenship?

⇨ What should the final report from the Commission say about citizenship and, in particular, post-16 citizenship?

⇨ What are you going to say to the Commission?

Professor Jonathon Tonge, the chair of the Commission, underlines the engagement of young citizens as an 'important challenge' in Britain. I am confident that it is one on which those involved in post-16 citizenship have much to contribute.
October 2008

⇨ The above information is reprinted with kind permission from National Foundation for Educational Research. Visit www.nfer.ac.uk for more information.

© National Foundation for Educational Research

⇨ In its simplest meaning, 'citizenship' is used to refer to the status of being a citizen – that is, to being a member of a particular political community or state. (page 1)

⇨ The Union Flag, or 'Union Jack', is the national flag of the United Kingdom and is so called because it embodies the emblems of the three countries united under one Sovereign – the kingdoms of England and Wales, of Scotland and of Ireland (although since 1921 only Northern Ireland, rather than the whole of Ireland, has been part of the United Kingdom). (page 2)

⇨ 76 per cent of people feel that they strongly belong to their neighbourhood with 81 per cent of people satisfied with their local area as a place to live. (page 6)

⇨ 39 per cent of people feel they can influence decisions affecting their local area. 22 per cent feel they could influence decisions affecting Great Britain. (page 6)

⇨ In the last decades of the twentieth century, there was a decline in the proportion of people in Great Britain who thought of themselves as primarily or exclusively British and a growing proportion of people who thought of themselves as Scottish, Welsh or English (or none of these) rather than British. (page 9)

⇨ Addressing deprivation and how people connect is more important for social cohesion than trying to get everyone to adhere to the same fixed notion of 'Britishness'. This is according to research published by the Joseph Rowntree Foundation. (page 10)

⇨ The 16- to 24-year-old focus group participants in the YouthNet study *Britain and beyond* were fairly ambivalent about being described as British and did not readily relate to a shared British identity. They were, however, conscious of the nations which made up the UK, both culturally and in terms of personal identity. (page 12)

⇨ A review published by the former attorney general Lord Goldsmith said that more than a third of young black Britons feel no sense of attachment to Britain, while a further one in ten people said they rejected all four identities of British, English, Scottish or Welsh. (page 13)

⇨ Since 1 November 2005 everyone that wants to permanently live in the UK has to take a test or attend citizenship and language classes to prove that they know about life in the UK. (page 15)

⇨ Over half of people (53%) have an interest in Parliament, although nearly as many (47%) have little or no interest. (page 16)

⇨ The Parliament of the United Kingdom consists of the House of Commons (646 elected Members of Parliament or MPs), the House of Lords (approximately 720 unelected members, most of them appointed for life and the Queen (our hereditary monarch). (page 17)

⇨ No new law can be made unless it has completed a number of stages in both the House of Commons and the House of Lords and has been signed by the monarch. A proposed new law is known as a Bill and can only become an Act of Parliament, and the law of the land, once it has completed all of its stages. (page 18)

⇨ The Government is chosen by the leader of the political party which has the majority of seats in the House of Commons. It is made up of about 100 MPs and members of the House of Lords who become government ministers. (page 20)

⇨ Voting turnout has dropped to record lows in recent general elections. (page 21)

⇨ Fair and free elections are an essential part of a democracy, allowing citizens to determine how they want the country to be governed. (page 22)

⇨ The electoral system used in the United Kingdom for elections to the House of Commons is the single member constituency with simple majority, also known as the first-past-the-post system. (page 24)

⇨ 61% of people surveyed by YouGov said it was very important that everyone votes in general elections, and 25% felt that it was fairly important. Only 3% felt it was not very or not at all important. (page 27)

⇨ A survey of its members aged between 14 and 25 by Girlguiding UK shows that they feel domestic violence, gangs and knife crime, bullying and workplace equality are the most important political issues for young women today. (page 33)

⇨ A petition is a list of names and basic details of people who support a particular issue or campaign. They are normally used to draw attention to a cause. Petitions highlight the level of support for the cause locally, nationally or internationally. (page 34)

⇨ Over 1.5 million 16- and 17-year-olds are denied the vote in the United Kingdom. (page 36)

⇨ Young people exhibit low levels of trust in politicians and political institutions, such as the European Union (EU). (page 38)

GLOSSARY

'Britishness'
There is currently much debate about our national identity: that is, what British values and identity are or should be, and whether they are still relevant. Aspects of the Britishness debate include whether Britishness and multiculturalism can co-exist; if we should have a national Britishness day to celebrate and encourage a shared identity, and whether compulsory citizenship ceremonies incorporating an oath of allegiance to the monarch should be compulsory for all British 18-year-olds.

Citizenship
A citizen is a legally-recognised national of a particular country. 'Citizenship' refers to a person's status as a citizen, but is also a much broader term encompassing the rights, responsibilities and duties of a citizen, such as social responsibility and voting in elections.

Constituency
The UK is divided up into 646 areas called constituencies. The voters in each constituency get to elect one MP to represent the people in their area in Parliament.

Democracy
A system of government where everyone living in a country has a say in who runs that country, typically through elections.

Devolution
Devolution refers to the granting of governing powers by a central government to the smaller government of a state or region. In the UK, for example, both Wales and Scotland have had devolved governments since September 1997. These are responsible for legislation covering just Wales or Scotland, while central government covers legislation relating to all of the UK. Some people feel that England should also be devolved.

Disengagement
Lack of involvement with politics and the running of the country, and with participation and citizenship in general. This may be the result of lack of interest, or be due to disillusionment with the political system.

Election
A vote which is held to choose someone to hold public office or other position. A general election takes place for people to decide which MP will represent them in parliament. A local election is held to give people the opportunity to determine who represents them on the local council.

First-past-the-post
The single member constituency with simple majority, also called first-past-the-post, is the electoral system used to decide the winners of elections in the UK. Put simply, this means that each voter has one vote and whichever candidate within their constituency gets the most votes becomes the MP for that region. The flaw in this is that even if 25,000 votes are cast against a candidate and only 20,000 are cast for them, they would still win the election as the 25,000 votes against would be divided between two or more other candidates.

Houses of Parliament
The British parliament buildings are the House of Commons and the House of Lords, both of which are in Westminster Palace in London. Elected politicians are known as MPs, which stands for Members of Parliament, each of whom represent a UK constituency and who meet regularly in the House of Commons for political debates and decision-making.

Mock election
A mock election is sometimes held to assess who people would elect if they were to vote in a general election. These are most often held among young people under the age of 18 and therefore not eligible to vote in national elections, to gauge their political opinions.

Multiculturalism
Multiculturalism refers to a society which consists of a number of groups with different customs and beliefs, all with equal status. Some people believe that adopting a policy of multiculturalism in Britain, rather than promoting a British national identity among its citizens, has led to increased racial and cultural segregation. However, others feel that it has enriched and diversified Britain to the benefit of all citizens.

Parliament
Many people confuse Parliament and Government. However, while the job of Government is to run the country, the job of Parliament is to check Government is carrying out its role properly and effectively. Parliament actually consists of three parts: the House of Commons, the House of Lords and the Queen. It is responsible for making and changing the laws of the United Kingdom as well as scrutinising the work of the Government.

Turnout
This refers to the number of people in the United Kingdom eligible to vote who actually turn out to vote in elections. In the past decade, turnout in general elections has fallen to a record low – only 61.3% of those eligible to do so voted in the last general election in 2005, compared with the 83.9% record voter turnout for the general election of 1950.

INDEX

Additional Resources

Other Issues titles

If you are interested in researching further some of the issues raised in *Citizenship and Participation*, you may like to read the following titles in the **Issues** series:

⇨ Vol. 172 *Racial and Ethnic Discrimination* (ISBN 978 1 86168 486 8)

⇨ Vol. 168 *Privacy and Surveillance* (ISBN 978 1 86168 472 1)

⇨ Vol. 167 *Our Human Rights* (ISBN 978 1 86168 471 4)

⇨ Vol. 149 *A Classless Society?* (ISBN 978 1 86168 422 6)

⇨ Vol. 147 *The Terrorism Problem* (ISBN 978 1 86168 420 2)

⇨ Vol. 142 *Media Issues* (ISBN 978 1 86168 408 0)

⇨ Vol. 137 *Crime and Anti-Social Behaviour* (ISBN 978 1 86168 389 2)

For more information about these titles, visit our website at www.independence.co.uk/publicationslist

Useful organisations

You may find the websites of the following organisations useful for further research:

⇨ **DCLG:** www.communities.gov.uk
⇨ **Directgov:** www.direct.gov.uk
⇨ **Electoral Reform Society:** www.electoral-reform.org.uk
⇨ **Hansard Society:** www.hansardsociety.org.uk
⇨ **HeadsUp:** www.headsup.org.uk
⇨ **Joseph Rowntree Foundation:** www.jrf.org.uk
⇨ **Ministry of Justice:** www.justice.gov.uk
⇨ **UK Parliament:** www.parliament.uk

ACKNOWLEDGEMENTS

The publisher is grateful for permission to reproduce the following material.

While every care has been taken to trace and acknowledge copyright, the publisher tenders its apology for any accidental infringement or where copyright has proved untraceable. The publisher would be pleased to come to a suitable arrangement in any such case with the rightful owner.

Chapter One: Identity and Belonging
What does citizenship mean?, © Citizenship Foundation, *National ceremonies and symbols*, © Crown copyright is reproduced with the permission of Her Majesty's Stationery Office, *'Moaning, drinking and queuing' make us British*, © Telegraph Group Ltd, London 2009, *A more United Kingdom*, © Demos, *Citizens feel a strong sense of belonging*, © Crown copyright is reproduced with the permission of Her Majesty's Stationery Office, *Citizenship: our common bond*, © Crown copyright is reproduced with the permission of Her Majesty's Stationery Office, *British identity*, © Crown copyright is reproduced with the permission of Her Majesty's Stationery Office, *Britishness and social cohesion*, © Joseph Rowntree Foundation, *A question of identity*, © The Herald, *Britain and beyond*, © YouthNet, *Just who do we think we are?*, © Kirsty Scott, *Citizenship tests*, © Hansard Society.

Chapter Two: Democracy in Action
Parliament and the public, © Hansard Society, *Discover Parliament*, © Crown copyright is reproduced with the permission of Her Majesty's Stationery Office, *Modern Britain 'needs Parliamentary reform'*, © Equality and Human Rights Commission, *Parliamentary elections*, © Crown copyright is reproduced with the permission of Her Majesty's Stationery Office, *Election jargon buster*, © Hansard Society, *Tackling voter disengagement*, © Electoral Reform Society, *Compulsory voting*, © Electoral Reform Society.

Chapter Three: Youth Participation
Are young people allergic to politics?, © Hansard Society, *Political outsiders?*, © Girlguiding UK, *Got a taste for it?*, © Electoral Commission, *The case for votes at 16*, © Votes at 16, *New evidence finds majority in favour of votes at 16*, © Votes at 16, *Votes at 16?* © openDemocracy. net, *Since citizenship arrived*, © National Foundation for Educational Research.

Photographs
Stock Xchng: pages 6 (Jerald Bernard); 8 (Phillip Bramble); 32 (Chris Chidsey); 36 (Steve Woods). **Wikimedia Commons:** pages 2 (Man vyi); 14 (NASA/ Bill Ingalls); 16 (David Iliff); 20 (Public domain).

Illustrations
Pages 1, 15, 25: Don Hatcher; pages 3, 29, 33: Angelo Madrid; pages 5, 9, 38: Simon Kneebone.

And with thanks to the team: Mary Chapman, Sandra Dennis, Claire Owen and Jan Sunderland.

Lisa Firth
Cambridge
May, 2009